MW01121946

SEARCHING WITHIN
A SPIRITUAL JOURNEY

Searching Within
A Spiritual Journey

By Doris Ann Bridgehouse

ISBN Number: 9781448693788

Cover and Book Design: Carol Pentleton/The Digital Artist
Copy editors: David Bridgehouse, Nancy Stanley,
            and Carol Pentleton
Photography: David and Doris Ann Bridgehouse

Website: www.numerologyusa.com

DEDICATION

I am grateful for the mysteries in life
that bind us together,
for loving people who have made my life full,
and the
two women who gave me the power
to speak from my heart,
my grandmother, Herminnie Boulé
and Aunt Mary Louise Vivian Halpin.

SPECIAL ACKNOWLEDGEMENT

In memory of Reverend Thomas E. Alhburn

We Remember You

Blue eyes - blue eyes
Bright and clear
You touched everyone with your gaze
Charmed in prose
Writing and speech
You centered yourself to be
Champion to the animals
Save a friend
Amuse the elderly
Practicing a purpose was your goal

Caring diligently
You plunged
Focused forward
Into life's dancing rhythm
With your tenacity and plan
Blessing us
In the present

Now caught in the web of timeless motion
You meet your season
We reach out
And our hearts respectively claim
A small corner of your space
Sending you love
Warm thoughts and wishes

Tom...
Listen – Listen
Silently listen
As we remember you.

TABLE OF CONTENTS

Chapter VI

Chapter VII

Part II
The Power of Understanding

Chapter VIII

Chapter IX

Chapter X

Chapter XI

Chapter XII

Part III
Stumbling Blocks

Chapter XIII

Chapter XIV

Chapter XV

Chapter XVI

Part IV
Harmony

Chapter XVII

Chapter XVIII

Chapter XIX

INTRODUCTION

On a spring day—about seventeen years ago—I began writing my experiences, insights, and philosophy in a daily journal. Soon the hypothesis of my writings mushroomed into a manuscript. With the help of my daughters, Rachel and Jessica, I categorized and segregated the endless notes into an outline. Later I entered those notes into the computer. For years I put the manuscript on the back burner until one winter morning. Entrenched in a twilight sleep, a thought provoked me to take pictures at Purgatory Chasm in Sutton, Massachusetts.

The Chasm is seventy feet high, a quarter of a mile long and filled with large tumbled boulders that nest between two secured granite walls. It is believed the Chasm was formed in the last Ice Age, approximately 14,000 years ago. This beautiful formation shows the power of the Netherworld—a mighty energy where limbo's emptiness welcomes individuals to enjoy nature either through meditation or play.

David, my husband, agreed the location would be a spectacular contrast of nature's profound strength against the melting snow. He added, "I think the Chasm pictures will help you to finish your book." David was right. Taking pictures at Purgatory Chasm swept me off my feet. I was in the "zone." I felt an extra jolt of energy and the whirl of life's magic.

The text shows the rewards of searching within one's heart and the rewards of empathic awareness—how to feel. Through a process of understanding our individuality and unique energy field, we are able to connect to a universal energy—a peaceful oneness. Depending on one's beliefs this is a connection to love/grace/God.

My epiphany to write the book came to me through an impromptu vision. I remember the day clearly as if it were yesterday. From an open window, a breeze provoked me to rise from an afternoon nap. With sleep in my eyes, I lazily took a deep breath. The smell of sprouting leaves, the aroma of growing grass, and the sweet scent of flowering trees made me think how the perfume of life is so intoxicating.

It was my day off from work and I felt like burrowing under the covers, but the guilt of unfinished housework gnawed at me. I was thinking of rolling out of bed when Annabelle, my cat, jumped on me. She purred and began kneading my leg. Half-heartedly I told her to get down. I had things to do and I could not sleep the day away like she.

Annabelle ignored my command. She circled, flopped in her space, and snuggled affectionately against my leg. Her expressive green eyes glowed with contentment. I did not have the energy to make her move. As her purring became louder, I knew she was on a mission. Annabelle magically had a sixth sense; she seemed to know when I needed to rest.

I said, "Okay Annabelle, I'll give into your summons. I'll relax, listen to your purr, and meditate."

I thought, she's right; nothing will fall apart by taking a few minutes to bond with my little friend. Moments later, while listening to her purr, I felt myself slipping into a tranquilized state. Swiftly, nature's spring aroma started to fuse into Annabelle's purr. My eyes felt heavy and soon fluttered shut. I could feel my senses expand. I began to witness a spiritual stillness. I thought this must be heaven. I did not have a care in the world.

Abruptly, a tapestry of soft colors of green, blue, brown, and white mixed with purple blended into one another until they formed the earth. To give the reader a reference, I describe the colors haphazardly for the colors are similar to those I described, but were unlike anything I have ever seen before. The earth pulsated—like a beating heart. Seawater swelled with glimmering foam. The forest illuminated an electric green color. Pink and purple hues draped the majestic mountains.

I felt dazed by the earth's immense power. Then as if looking at an aerial photograph, I saw the earth against a backdrop of darkness strewn with brilliant stars. The darkness seemed alive and commanding. The stars twinkled with waves of energy and light. It was fascinating to see how the earth, the darkness, and the stars had their own distinctive qualities—their contrast to one another morphed into a uniqueness that formed a whole.

Suddenly, I felt as though I was floating among the stars. The beauty of the earth and the universe's boundlessness felt overwhelming. Involuntary tears of joy streamed from my eyes. I was consumed mentally and physically by the vision.

Without reason, everything turned dark—deeper than the color black. I felt anxious. An unknown force kept me frozen while it pulled me deeper into an obscure place. I struggled to break away from this hypnotic state, but the darkness secured me with a forceful grip. I could see nothing. There was nothing in my life to hold onto. The nothingness felt final. It seemed that all my experiences in life were unreal; my life as I knew it was a pretense.

I had no family or friends. There was no beauty or ugliness. The harder I tried to oppose the vision the deeper the darkness envelopment me. I found I could no longer measure or compare something to anything else. There was absolutely nothing—nothing at all. I felt disappointed and empty. My body involuntarily shivered. For a while the darkness kept me blank, as blank as the darkness.

Finally, I surrendered to my uneasiness. I asked myself, "What is the purpose to life? Where am I in this empty dark space?"

Instantaneously, a surge of love and strength connected to a fulfilling oneness enveloped my mind and body. This love—oneness—was not a belief nor did it have an image.

When I released my anxiety and opened myself a loving energy, the darkness was absorbed and everything turned into an aurora-borealis-like luminosity. The multicolored lights transmuted into one another with a force of deliberation. After the lights entwined themselves, they broke away from one another and started the ritual again. Through observation, I saw that neither light was better or brighter than another. If anything, each movement looked like the beginning and the ending of a grand dance.

In the distance, I felt Annabelle softly touch my face with her paw. When I did not react, she placed her wet nose on mine. This was a habit of hers to receive my undivided attention. I promptly opened my eyes. She walked on my chest to make sure I was fully awake, and then jumped off the bed.

I stretched and took a deep breath to pull in the warm spring air. I felt invigorated. I had a new outlook on life. All beings, whether sentient or animate, have their own separateness, yet they are joined together. Now I try to embrace the sleeping golden moments where the unexpected lies and observe myself through life's sacred existence.

PART I
LIFE'S ENERGY FLOW

REDEMPTION

You live in the froth of indignation
Trying to breathe the air of yesterday
The air you will never breathe again
Doubt, shame, and fear
Surround your soul

Hear the call
Reach beyond your grasp
Search beyond your mind
Turn your dreams back
Before the beginning of time
Between shadowed days
Take a moment
Clear and still
To touch your inner spirit

It is here you will find a happy middle-ground
That ripples and expands
Transforming,
Shaping, and improving
Your life by conscious demand.

·

Chapter I

Humor keeps you in a state of grace.

The Beginning

An insight began years ago when a friend invited me to lunch. We had fallen out of touch, and I looked forward to catching-up. I waited for her patiently. As usual, she was late. Twenty minutes later she walked toward me. She looked at her watch and waved. I smiled. She smiled back, but I saw tears welling in her eyes.

She told me she had a horrible weekend. She complained about how her future mother-in-law excluded her and her daughter from being part of a family portrait. I touched her hand and felt her pain as though her experience was mine.

Following the incident, I periodically sensed the physical condition and essence of others. Those intimate moments made me feel muddled. Sometimes, to my chagrin, I wept uncontrollably about people's tragedies and life's injustices. With the uncertainty of not knowing or understanding where I began and where someone else ended, I became fearful.

From the vision with Annabelle, I knew I had to let go of my so-called convictions. I broke away from that in between feeling by meditating. As my heart opened—whether comfortable or uncomfortable—I engaged in dialogue. I observed my reaction to situations—especially if someone irritated me. I wrote daily snippets in the squares on a calendar. Sometimes I wrote something wise; sometimes I tripped over my words. These small gestures helped me to find meaning in my surroundings. I replaced negative thoughts with positive affirmations, and gained a new stamina. I slowly felt safe in my own skin—I was home.

Today, my spirit is layered with other people's spirits. I honor those who have helped me to become more than I was before. Yes, I still question myself. Yes, there are moments I feel insecure. However, the difference between now and then is I know when I feel doubtful. I am not as likely to react out of fear. It is through the sense of self I recognized the universal energy—love/grace/God.

NURTURING ONE'S ENERGY FIELD

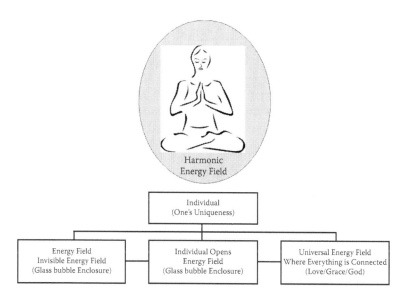

Think of everything as a conduit of energy and at birth each person has an energy field surrounding his or her body—a personal harmonic vibration. This harmonic vibration represents the dimensions of our existence. It gives us solace when we feel uncomfortable and alerts us to danger. When we are aware of our harmonic energy field, we automatically connect to a higher energy source—a vast openness— a place where one joins with nature and all life forms.

Imagine that you are—your individuality—enclosed in a glass bubble. This bubble represents an invisible energy force that separates your uniqueness from others. Your energy is under your control. On the other side of the glass bubble enclosure, other individuals live similarly. Their harmonic energy field cannot be penetrated unless one allows it.

Consider this openness a bridge to a higher consciousness where regeneration, healing, and spiritual evolutionary growth excel—placing you in the state of love/grace/God. It is here one feels the fullness of life.

The opposite of openness is constricted energy. One feels isolated until one consciously opens his or her enclosed glass bubble; Notice how you feel when you are at odds with the world. There is separateness where one is inclined to exert an unhealthy attitude toward life. It will not matter if you are involved in a loving relationship, running successful business, busy completing deadlines, or have oodles of money in the bank. The frustration from the separateness feels like banishment.

In this phase, one's energy shrivels. This also happens when something negative is deprived of energy—it has little chance to grow. For example, a houseplant requires sunlight, water, and attention. The same concept applies to sentient beings. Individuals who live with an angry undertone, are self-absorbed, lie, cheat, betray people's trust, and respond to situations with cruelty are unknowingly harming themselves. They cannot feel life's oneness.

There is only way to free oneself from this tortured place; live in the moment. Do not torment yourself with unhappy notions by wishing the present moment would change. Do not live in the past—for your interpretations from the past are flawed. Do not get stuck in the future. Anticipation will not bring about transformation. A clear positive intention in the present moment gravitates toward its own fulfillment; activating an alteration to the future.

Feel it. The energy flow has a special silence—a particular type of stillness. It connects to your kindred spirit—your life's flame. Remember how it feels to have fun—the cheers and the laughter. You would not consider those positive sounds noisy. There are no noises with general dialogue, with genuine caring, with sharing, or positive intent. The energy flow moves forward with support and balance.

What are noisy energy sounds? An empathic person hears an obtrusive distorting sound. It feels something like an uncomfortable whirling hum. This happens with superficial gestures of kindness, relentless chattering, deceit, or manipulation. Listen to the sound of anger, the sound of hate, and the sound of revenge. Can you hear those noisy sounds? Become aware of the sounds in your surroundings and the sounds you make in your own life.

Example: Distorting Life's Energy Flow

John had a miserable day at the office and by the end of the day he was exhausted. He could not wait to leave his building. As he was closing his office door, the telephone rang. In the interim, his new secretary, Carrie, answered the telephone. A client needed directions to his office.

Since Carrie was not familiar with the city's geography, she called]to John and asked him to give the client directions. Abruptly, he cursed under his breath and snatched the telephone from her hand. The telephone call did not warrant this type of behavior. John depleted his energy flow. His negativity could only affect Carrie if she allows his actions to enter her harmonic energy field.

I think this perspective is one of the most difficult aspects of life's journey to understand. Let me reiterate. John's negative response broke the connection to the universal energy flow—his connection to Carrie. His energy field collapses into itself—depleting his energy. Carrie making a conscious choice by refusing to be part of John's energy field will keep her in the universal energy flow.

When one practices awareness, it is easy to follow the best path. Respect and compassion for another human being's vibration allows another's energy field to flow through you. If John chose to thank his secretary for an honest days work, he would have felt mentally and physically better and had all the energy he needed.

Exercise:

The universe constantly gives us second chances. We can always begin again—though differently. Before you start on a freedom quest, you must understand the condition of your emotional vulnerability and the quality of your responses to others. Here are four exercises. They may help you recognize the present moment.

•Grasp the moment and speak the truth.

•Reassess your motives.

•When necessary, apologize for you own indiscretions. If you feel others have made a mistake, let it go.

•Make a deliberate attempt to be helpful. It does not matter who a person is as much as why a special gesture feels right.

EMPATHIC AWARENESS

Empathic awareness is a highly evolved state. It is a place of equanimity. Empathic people are inspirationally active and spontaneous. They are in-tune with their emotions and have self-understanding. They feel another person's frustrations but they are not an emotional sponge—which would wear down their spirit. If they feel a pressure or heaviness around them, they project a warm comforting light. They mentally and physically will not allow life's upheavals to distort an experience

Think of this analogy. There are two ways to view natural light. On a damp and cloudy day, the majority of people may view the day as somewhat gloomy. But when the sun shines through the clouds, individuals tend to view the day as uplifting. Empathic people do not set the stage of life by appearances. They know life's daily routine or new plateaus are merely another facet to living.

They realize their desires, personal beliefs, and ideas belong to their spiritual path. They would never project those beliefs onto others. They live in the moment where time does not exist. An empathic person knows they cannot fix anyone's problems or make someone feel fulfilled. One cannot strive to become empathic anymore than one can attempt to be honest. One is either open to being part of another person or he or she is not.

Exercise:
Look into a mirror—if possible a full-length mirror. Inhale deeply. Exhale gently through your mouth. Touch the contour of your face. Observe and describe your face in detail with a positive outlook. Speak out loud as if you were beholding your face for the first time. Look at the texture of your skin, hair, and neck. Look at your clothing. What is the texture of your clothing? What colors are you wearing?

Name one element about yourself that is unlike anyone else. Inhale deeply. Exhale again. The person in the mirror is the person you are right now. Specifically notice you are not an image of anyone else.

Through this simple exercise, you will learn how it feels to be empathic. Practice this exercise daily until you feel comfortable. At that point, you will realize observing another person is similar to observing yourself.

While you were looking in the mirror, did divisive thoughts float into your head? If so, dissect those thoughts. Think of them as three levels of understanding. I call the levels C words: Control, Conflict, and Change. Letting go of control depletes conflict, and opens you to the infinite world of change.

CHAPTER II

Simple decisions make huge impacts.

CONTROL

Anytime you want to control a situation you are exercising authority. This action is fear based. It shows you fail to trust and you are frightened of the unknown. To recognize your control issues, pay close attention to the images in your mind. Are they creative or are they restricting? How do they make you feel mentally and physically?

Example 1: Control by Being Ignored
Marlene has been dating her boyfriend, Chuck, for three months. The rub is Chuck happens to take Marlene on dates where his best friend Carolyn will be (she is either alone or with a friend). He invites her to join them, and then proceeds to ignore Marlene for the rest of the evening.

She told me her boyfriend is respectful and kind toward Carolyn. Her eyes filled with tears as she mentioned she rarely receives the same treatment. At a family gathering, Marlene's sister mentioned to Chuck how Marlene felt.

Chuck was upset with Marlene for sharing her thoughts with her sister. He subsequently accused her of being petty, insecure, and jealous of Carolyn.

Obviously, Marlene has been pushed to the wall. This is her defining moment. Over the past six months she has been a good sport—bordering on being a doormat. Only Marlene can break this crooked path. It is up to her to be the captain of her ship. She has a choice—live with the problem or make a change in the relationship.

Example 2: Control, Intense Situation

Mary Louise moved into her, boyfriend, Carlton's home five months ago with her puppy, Gray. Cynthia, Mary Louise's best friend, also had a puppy named Cuddles. From the beginning, Cynthia and Mary Louise scheduled a day once a week for the puppies to play. This ritual went on for ten months.

Carlton thought he would surprise Mary Louise with a seven-month old rescued German Shepard named Tiny. As a puppy, he was crated and alone most of the time; consequently, he lacked social skills. Tiny was confrontational with Gray and Cuddles and he had to be disciplined often.

Since Tiny came aboard, Carlton's attitude with the dogs changed drastically. Every time the dogs were disorderly Carlton became intense and used foul language. Mary Louise and Cynthia said and did nothing. They thought if they did not question Carlton, he would change. The next few weeks were much the same. The dogs would become unruly; Carlton would curse. Soon Cynthia and Cuddles would gracefully go home.

Carlton is a man that feeds off the passivity of others. In order for him to feel in control, he reacts negatively to a situation. He knows by being obnoxious and boisterous Cynthia will leave the premises.

Cynthia explained to Mary Louise she cannot tolerate Carlton's demeanor any longer. She told Cynthia she will visit her when Carlton is unavailable, otherwise they can find another location for Gray and Cuddles to play.

Mary Louise chooses to overlook Carlton explosive behavior. She makes excuses for him to numb her feelings and to get by the snags and snarls of her unstable relationship. If she opened herself to what is, she would realize her unhealthy misstep, and be able to change her direction in life (see Chapter VII, "What Love is Not").

Example 3: Control, Living in Limbo

I am at the age where many of my friends, including myself, have health issues. After a mammogram exam the radiologists noted there was a lump in my left breast. It was either pre-cancer or cancer. A biopsy had to be done. As anyone could imagine, waiting for the diagnosis placed me in limbo. I began living in my head of what might be —allowing the ego to produce negative thoughts.

I broke the ego's control by observing the tension I was putting myself in. I kept busy with positive actions. As negative thoughts rose, I rubbed my hands together until they were warm, and then I shook them away from me. I mediated and allowed my spirit to guide me to wonderful people. They gave me a tremendous peace. Nature also grounded me.

If you find yourself in limbo, follow your heart, express yourself to others and observe the wonder in each moment. As it turned out, the mammogram showed a false positive. I did not have a lump after all.

Questions:
Are you aware of your surroundings? Do you feel comfortable in your own skin? Are you under stress? If so, take a deep breath and envelop your body with a stream of white light.

•You are the only one who can find your key to peace.

CONFLICT

Conflict means a clash of ideas—in opposition—or a contradiction of how we think something should or could be. No matter how trivial or insignificant our circumstances conflict binds us into an obsessive frenzy and perpetuates itself into a non-ending crisis—causing emotional turmoil and helplessness.

When we experience conflict, our ego eludes the truth and inserts a false belief. Since no one enjoys living in a tortuous state, we try to relieve ourselves from the torment by attempting to transfer our conflicts onto others. We do not see that our conflicts reside in our own psyche.

Breaking away from the chokehold of control and conflict, we will no longer resemble the caged hamster on a churning wheel—going nowhere fast. By conquering the duality of conflict, we are able to accept change—something conflict cannot do.

Example: Control, Conflict, and Change

Echo has been working for the same employer for ten years. For the past three years, she feels her position is complete drudgery. She thinks she should further her education in order to receive a promotion. But every school semester Echo plans on enrolling in an evening class she vacillates with the thought she dislikes driving during the evening. In her heart, she knows she needs to stimulate her mind and now is the time to enhance her creative skills. She feels rattled by her tumbling thoughts. She asks herself, "Why can't I just sit back and enjoy my life?"

Echo has two voices speaking to her. One voice is like a mature and rational parent. The second voice is her inner child, who seeks change, wonder, and adventure. Both parent and child must meet in the middle—where the universal energy flows.

How can Echo find relief from her conflict? The initial solution is to take one small step. Observe one's thoughts without wishing and wanting, and then watch conflicts unravel like a skein of yarn.

The second and last step is to take physical action. After all, we live in the physical world. Echo needs to understand the essence of her creative and subconscious mind. She could make a list of the plusses and minuses she receives from her position. Try thinking outside the box; possibly, take a course on a Saturday morning. This small gesture will give her a sense of accomplishment and help her get back into a studying mode.

No one knows how one will feel about anything until one does something about it. Once the chain of conflict is broken, one gains strength to explore the undiscovered— dismantling the hidden.

Exercise:

Everyone experiences feelings of uncertainty. Look at those forces as something positive for they are an opening to awareness. Take a moment to find a quiet place in your home and listen to the voices that consume your thoughts. Make it a habit to concentrate on positive thoughts for a few minutes to help your inner child move forward.

As negative thoughts float through your mind, such as, "I am fat and no one likes me...add... I love myself and others love me also." Repeat as needed. Also, melt away subliminal negative messages with an affirmation. Note that it takes many positive affirmations to replace one negative message.

Here are a few affirmations: I love myself. I make joyous decisions. I deserve positive recognition. For those who feel inventive, create your own affirmation. Do not hurry affirmations, and always recite them with deep sincerity.

Try this exercise daily. You will feel stronger and your conflict will become weaker. Understand your conflict is your subjective viewpoint; you are your opinion. You are the one tying yourself in knots. Do not allow control and conflict to deplete your energy.

THE EGO

Our egos help us to survive in the physical world—keeping us balanced. But when there is too much ego, it blocks everything else that is dear to us and makes us vulnerable and fragile. Through disappointment and impermanence we allow the ego to control us. It invades the truth and hoards and clings to keep our problems alive. The ego cannot show love, exhibit kindness, or compassion.

Watch your ego as it wars with itself and scuffles with reality—frazzling you. It is in this swirling expectation state that the ego twists your perception to further its demands. Making you think as soon as you get around the corner the future will hold happiness.

Life rightly begins by practicing mindfulness. Do not allow the ego to rule you through a past concept. The past is a subjective memory that seduces you—whirling you in circles as if you were a spinning top. Remember, as soon as you try to project an outcome you will lose a peacefulness that is contained in equanimity. Experience the eternal new where there are no trappings or assumptions to cloud your judgments.

If perchance something does not turn out as you had hoped, step into the truth of the matter—and allow your harmonic energy field and the universal energy flow to catapult you toward a higher spiritual level. By doing this, the ego will slip into its proper place.

Enjoy the opportunities and wonderful moments in front of you without dwelling that they should be grander than they are. Become transparent. And tap into the openness of love. It never disappoints.

Example 1: Ego, Refocus
Let us pretend Sally, a neighbor's child, notices you gardening in the back yard. She walks toward you bubbling about her experience in the school play yard. You think, "Sally is adorable, but right now I just want to plant my flowers."

Two sentences into Sally's story, you feel she is taking too long explaining her experience. You interrupt and finish Sally's sentence wishing she would hurry and go away. Soon Sally instinctively knows you are trying to rush her; you see sadness in her enormous hazel eyes. The ego tries to bamboozle you into thinking other people feelings or thoughts are unnecessary.

Refocus! Learn to enjoy a spontaneous moment. You could explain to Sally you would love to hear all about her experience, but right now you are in the middle of planting and watering your flowers. Ask her to come back in a half hour. Tell her how you will have milk and cookies ready for her return. Do not miss the opportunity to join in Sally's wonder. By explaining yourself honestly, both you and another person are able to appreciate each other's space.

Example 2: Ego, Impatience
Let us suppose what you thought would be a quick errand became a twenty minute wait in the grocery store line. Later, at the main intersection, there was a traffic jam, and now you are late for an important appointment. You tried calling the receptionist to mention you were running late, but an automated telephone system placed you on hold.

Your heart begins to race and your impatience rises to an aggravating level. At this point, your ego questions your self-worth; placing you in conflict. You wished you did not go to the grocery store. You wished you left earlier. You hate everyone involved in the traffic jam. You hate yourself.

Find balance. Learn a lesson from your experience. Change your attitude. Wishing or being impatient is a waste of time. Stay in the moment and take advantage of the traffic jam. Notice your surroundings. Take deep breaths and listen to your breathing. The payment for impatience is aggravation. Relaxation is free. Enjoy the reward.

Exercise:
When the ego is in control, you become irritated. To help you focus, practice saying a one word affirmation. Surround yourself with a favorite color (see Chapter XVIII "Nature's Natural Colors"). Or place a small treasured object in your pocket and hold on to it whenever your tensions build. Think of your own antidote—any positive gesture will take you to a better place.

Beliefs

A belief is a conviction or an acceptance that certain things are true. The tricky part of the equation is humans want to believe in something. We gravitate toward ideas that make us feel safe, and then measure and judge others against the belief.

We do not have to think alike to get along with each other. And when we are self-absorbed with a belief system, we are neither interesting nor persuasive. Actually, we are dismissing our spirit and giving the ego the lead.

We cannot force our personal beliefs on anyone anymore than we can convince someone that his or her beliefs are false. Diverse cultures and diverse ideas make sentient beings interesting. Sharing each other's beliefs is like being part of giant web—each strand is as important as another.

I weigh the fact that if one's belief separates or renounces his or her connection to others there is something amiss. I think showing bias toward a belief is like pushing a door bell. It must yammer the same boring jingle. Do you recognize a belief system with the examples below?

Examples:

1. Perfection

Some people live their life as if they were playing fictional characters in a movie—looking for perfection. If someone thinks you are supposed to be perfect, it is his or her problem. If you expect someone to be perfect, it is your problem.

2. Wedding or Any Social Function

How many people have told you their social celebration has to be perfect? Let me quote a friend. "I am spending a fortune on my daughter's wedding. I know how to do it right."

This belief is relative. There are no correct procedures to celebrate a wedding. The validity of a social function cannot be measured by how much money is spent, the locality of the function, or how many guests attend. One cannot put a price tag on sharing or having a good time.

3. Neighborhood

Two people from a neighborhood form a relationship even though they have dissimilar religious beliefs; their moral practices are the same.

4. Relatives

Family members have opposing viewpoints. They meet in the middle and agree not to debate about each other's particular beliefs. They recognize family functions should be a place filled with love and peace.

5. Illness

A family member becomes ill. The relatives bond together, even though their belief system is broadly based. They create a partnership to selflessly help their family member.

6. Career Couples

When both partners work full time, there is an obligation to share the household workload.

Example: Beliefs

Mariah's parents were strict and adamant about her dating habits. She was raised to date only young men from her own nationality and religious background. Mariah met Alexander through her older brother, Eddy.

Throughout high school, Alexander and Mariah dated in a restricted environment. They either met at her home or visited his parents. They rarely went on traditional dates; if so, someone in the family would tag along.

While in college their relationship progressed. Mariah and Alexander became physically intimate. They were together for two years until Alexander became super possessive.

In the beginning of their relationship, Mariah enjoyed Alexander's jealous attentions. She thought it was cute, but his jealousy escalated and he became frighteningly aggressive. He would verbally abuse her and she was afraid of him. Ultimately, she ended their relationship.

Mariah met Todd through her friend, Heather. She enjoyed Todd's company. He had a variety of interests and he was not as clingy as Alexander. He told Mariah he cared for her, immensely, although he could only see her two days a week due to his heavy workload and studies.

After seven months of dating, Mariah broke up with him. Her family was delighted she ended her relationship with Todd. They told her she should go back to Alexander. He was a good prospect and they knew he still loved her. Eventually, she caved into her parent's demands. Her friends tried to convince her to wait before she made such a drastic decision. After all, she had plenty of time to meet someone new. And they reminded her of the reason she broke up with Alexander in the first place.

Mariah must recognize she is the only one who can pave the road to her happiness. And leaning on someone else's opinion—parents or otherwise—will not ensure a fulfilling future.

Questions:

Do you practice your belief through love or fear? Do your beliefs give you solace?

•Take the role you play in life seriously. Beliefs are all well and good; however they must be put to a test before they can show their true value.

Chapter III

*Put yourself in line for new experiences,
and then allow life to unfold.*

Change

Change means a complete obliteration of an opinion or the replacement of a past pattern. Most of us tend to think of change, and especially unforeseen change, as negative. We like our space to remain intact unless we are in control. Even people living under intolerable conditions will resist change.

Recognize the contrasting layers of change. For instance, chronological change is inevitable; everything in this world disappears—eventually. One does not have to be attentive or alert to experience this type of change. A marriage, a birth, illness, a promotion, a job loss, or growing old are common life experiences.

The second part to change is the change we make from within. For instance: how one views a feeling, how one reacts to adversity, or how one understands his or her life.

Those changes cannot be ignored. They make one feel alive.

Years ago, I saw a friend of mine in a grocery store. I asked him, "How has life been treating you?"

He sighed, "My company downsized and I was terminated."

I gave him a hug and told him I was so sorry. He told me as of yesterday he was feeling better; he had a revelation.

He shrugged his shoulders in a lackadaisical manner. He said, "I guess the universe is telling me I should be working somewhere else."

I was shocked. This person had a tendency to be narrow minded. His transformation was bound to take him to a new place. A place he would have never thought of exploring.

CHANGE UNFOLDING

As life's changes unfold, hidden issues unveil themselves. Change, control, conflict, worry, and frustration—which are familiar positions—hamper the here-and-now. By understanding and accepting unfolding changes there is a release connected to an unlimited energy. This energy will surely improve your senses and guide you toward clarity. The tricky part of change you must be careful not to replace one dogmatic action for another.

Here is an analogy. Observe how your feet feel. Think of them as a reflection of your life right now. Do your shoes feel too tight? Do your toes hurt? Are you getting a blister?

Evaluate your life. Maybe it is time to look for a better fit, elsewhere. Do not allow a few ache or pains to discourage you. If you trip along the way or repeat the same mistake—so what. Now is the time to improve your approach.

Besides, repeating a gesture over could become the break-through you were looking for. In the path to openness, there are no wrong decisions.

Exercise:
For one month, daily write in a journal. This exercise will help you to learn how to observe life's massive panorama. After the month has passed, read what you have written. Do you see your experiences from a multifarious viewpoint?

TRAUMATIC CHANGE

Traumatic changes have a strange power. They may kill one's passion or alter life's essences. This could be through a sudden death of a loved one, a severe accident, a debilitating health issue, or a betrayal. Also, being a victim of a crime certainly is a traumatic change.

Sometimes victims blame themselves thinking they could have made a better choice, placed themselves in another location, or could have done something different to eradicate their circumstance. They fail to consider some traumatic changes are random.

Through this type of change a person may create a narrow world and isolate him or herself from others—which ultimately will direct a person further into isolation. There are no easy answers to relieve one from this type of pain. Because our harmonic energy fields are so diversified it is impossible to give one concrete answer for everyone.

If a traumatic event has happened to you, you have my deepest sympathy. My heart goes out to anyone whose life has taken them down a bleak path. I truly hope someone will be able to guide you to a place where you can retrieve your light. Never feel ashamed to ask a relative, an intimate friend, clergy or perhaps a qualified psychoanalyst to help.

Be aware that your trauma will feed on your weaknesses and it will continually perpetuate itself until you put a stop to it. Understand you are your own best control, as well as the source of your own conflict. When you live in the present, the stagnant energy around you—the past—will release you to an opening and deliver you to what is.

ACCEPTING "WHAT IS"

Accepting "what is" is similar to walking through a maze. As one enters a maze, he or she may feel confused and befuddled. But as one proceeds forward an ease develops where one wholeheartedly joins with an answer—striking the words would, should or could have been from his or her vocabulary.

Once at this level, an individual will shed off frustration and vagueness. Do not allow anything to be in direct competition with one another. Figure out which you want more, and give up all things opposing it. Realize throughout life's journey, there is no such thing as being obstacle-free, annoyance free, or that it is possible to possess an idiot-free existence. At the hub of the action, you are bound to find truth of what is.

Example 1: What is, Accident

Jackie has been an athlete since she was seven years old. In high school, she played on a championship varsity lacrosse team. She enjoyed the notoriety of the winning team and all the benefits that went with it. Unfortunately, three weeks before the play-offs she severely broke her leg.

Her prognosis: After Jackie's leg heals she will need extensive physical therapy. She will never be able to play sports again. Depression took hold of Jackie's heart. She felt her life was nonexistant and she continually blamed herself for the accident. Since she was not mentally clear, she made a decision to become intimate with an acquaintance—even through she did not care for him. Her indulgence placed her in a worse mental state.

Jackie ought to stop punishing herself and question her actions. Are her choices lifting her up or adding to her troubles? Is she going to allow the bondage connected to life's disappointments control her or is she going to discover another vision for herself?

Honesty is important. She will have to search within and ask her spirit how to honor her harmonic energy field. She is at a crossroad where challenges point to a beginning. It is up to her to make a new life for herself.

Example 2: What Is, Choice

May has been living with her boyfriend, Courtland, for eight years. Last December after a deep discussion they agreed to take their relationship to the next level. Courtland, at last, asked May to marry him.

One evening she read Courtland a newspaper health article. It mentioned that married people are less stressed, had lower blood pressure, etc. He responded by saying he did not feel stressed unless he counted the stress of being forced into marriage.

May was dumbfounded. She confronted Courtland. He told her he was only joking. She felt insulted and returned the engagement ring. After a few weeks passed, she tried to have a serious dialogue with Courtland about the incident. But every time she approached him, he either avoided the issue by making a joke or quickly changed the subject. She wonders why he has not re-asked her to marry him.

Maybe it is time she acknowledges what is. Even though she has had an eight year investment in the relationship, Courtland has not slipped the ring back on her finger. Sad to say, the present moment indicates it is time she took an intermission from her dreams.

Courtland has a right to make his choice—even though it was capped with a mean spirited sense of humor. May should not waste a moment giving into his emotional bidding or analyze his subconscious motives. The present moment speaks for itself.

Exercise:

Question the one thing that you wish you could change. While you are questioning yourself, search within—dig deep. How do you feel? Are you living your life by resisting "what is?" Note the answer is in your question.

CHAPTER IV

*An evolved person hears the music
connected to a moment.*

LISTENING

The art of listening depends on our quality of life—physically and spiritually. It is the only way to sprout wings, and no longer feel bound by the forces that keep us down.

But before I address listening to others, I want to point out the bombarding thoughts that come into our heads randomly. Do the thoughts you hear control you?

If so, take a deep breath a couple of times to quiet your mind. Search within. Practice meditation techniques (see Chapter XIX, "Meditation and Space"). It is not so much one has to get to a place as to realize it takes many avenues to get there. This happens by listening. How else can one quantify something, or improve it?

There is nothing more refreshing than sharing a perspective in someone else's world and letting the interpretations of that person's views unfold. Healthy dialogue gives us a chance to digest new ideas and throw away antiquated notions. Dialogue implicates a sharing and a letting go. Transcend and feel another's spiritual light. Realize each step you take affects a part of your personal growth, and it all begins by simply listening.

Blind listening is when individuals speak to each other without either person listening. Egoistically, they stroke their own viewpoint. There is no growth. No opening. No contact.

Example 1: Listening, Pet Peeve

Joan and Jack love each other dearly, but they both have a pet peeve that is extinguishing the flame in their relationship. John likes to keep the temperature in their apartment cool. Joan likes it to be relatively warm. Since they are at the opposite side of a temperature threshold—especially through the winter months—their relationship shrinks into an emotional turmoil.

They waste their precious energy by scuffling over the position of who is right and who is in the wrong. Daily they descend on the same negative reactionary merry-go-round. They do not realize they are neglecting their love for each other.

When individuals open themselves to feel one another's spirits—empathic awareness—it is easier to resolve a solution. In this sacred place, one is not fragmented with subjective sensitivities. Realize where there is love and respect there is an answer.

Example 2: Listening to One's Needs

On Memorial Day, both Jane and Ann were invited to a friend's late afternoon picnic. Ann volunteered to drive Jane. Jane felt they should take separate cars since she had to be at work at the next morning at 6:00 a.m. Jane knew

Ann was a night owl; she made it explicitly clear she did not want to ruin Ann's fun by leaving the party early. Ann told Jane they would leave the party as soon as she gave her the "it is time to go sign." Jane mentioned she would like to leave the party around eleven o'clock.

At 10:50, Jane tapped Ann on the shoulder and whispered she felt worn-out. She was ready to go home. Ann begged Jane to compromise. She told Jane she was having such a great time she hated the thoughts of leaving the party right now.

She smiled and made a gesture crossing her heart. She jokingly replied, "I'll be like Cinderella, I promise to leave the party at midnight."

Jane felt pushed into a corner. She rolled her eyes and made it clear she was not happy with their new arrangement, but for the sake of their friendship, she said okay. When the clock struck midnight, Ann told Jane she would like to stay one more hour. She reiterated to Jane that she hated to leave the party when she was having so much fun.

Ann gave Jane a light hug and smiled sheepishly with a comment, "After all, what is the big deal. You are only losing a few hours sleep."

Jane is aware of her reality. She is the person who had to get up early. Jane listened to Ann; she sensed how much Ann did not want to leave the party. Jane gave into Ann's demand, again. She did not want Ann to be upset with her.

Later that evening, Ann teased Jane in front of their friends. She told the group Jane was a baby whining about losing a few hours sleep and she was a fuddy-duddy. The rest of the evening Jane felt uneasy. She realized Ann was not interested in listening to her. Their relationship was not the relationship she thought it was. The situation, although painful, liberated Jane from her illusion.

Example 3: Listen to Self

A woman and her boyfriend were to be married in five months. They had a conversation about the possibility of having children someday. She wants children. He does not.

Later he decided that it would be okay for them to have a child, but she would have to lose weight. Because of her medical history, she agreed it was a good idea. Then the other day he told her the real reason they should not have children. He thought she would make a lousy mother since she did not drive safely or cook well.

She went on to explain. She has never been in an automobile accident. She admits she is not the best cook, but she does do most of the household chores and yard work.

Having a child with this man sounds like a fate far worse than being alone. Fill me in. What do his issues have to do with mothering? He does not respect his fiancée. He changes everything around to be her fault. I ask: how can someone who is supposed to love his fiancée treat her with such contempt?

Example 4: Listening, Being Reasonable

Secondhand smoke poses a significant health risk to everyone, especially children. However, one cannot control what someone else chooses to do in their home. But in one's own home an individual may find smoking in their presence offensive. The person who smokes needs to listen and review his or her behavior to honor the essence of another's harmonic energy field. Do not become estranged due to the lack of consideration.

Exercise 1:

Practice gazing into an individual's eyes. Look deeply. Listen with your ears and heart. Listen to how a person responds to you? Do you interrupt a person while he or she is speaking? Do not allow your mind to wander. Does confusion choke your openness?

Whenever you are not clear about what someone is expressing to you, communicate that fact.

Exercise 2:

Try a new approach by making a fresh start. Relate to a person that makes you feel uneasy. Be vulnerable for a moment. Ask this person an interesting question; a question that will have a profound meaning for both of you—not a question with a yes or no answer. Listen to yourself as you ask the question. Listen with all your being. If you feel tense, wear an elastic band on your wrist and snap it whenever you lose your bearings.

How do you feel before, during, and after the question? Did you let go of your presupposed ideas? Did the individual give careful consideration to your question? Did the individual act kind toward you? Did you stay in the moment?

Relationships are connected experiences, the deeper your dialogue the more satisfying your relationships become. If perchance, your dialogue went nowhere and you still do not resonate with this person. It is okay, you tried. And the experience is bound to open you to a new way of thinking.

ASSUMING

People live in their heads and assume all sorts of things. When you assume anything, realize you do not know. There is only one way to know anything—investigate. Do not live a life of what may be; live a life of what is. Break the habit of assuming. Sit in silence. Observe yourself. Ask your spirit to push through your ego's foolishness and connect to the moment where peace resides.

Example 1: Assuming, Questioning Relationship

A friend of mine has been dating her guy for three years. Through their relationship, he has been very attentive. He texts her often, or calls her out of the blue. Then six weeks ago he asked her to visit his parents and meet his son. She was in heaven.

Since then he has not returned her calls. Recently they saw each other at a mutual friend's home and he hardly acknowledged her. She thought he appeared spaced out. She is freaking out. She does not know if she should make an effort to back off or reframe from going to their old haunts.

I feel one should never assume. It is best she confronts him personally (not by telephone or text messaging). Tell him the truth. Mention how much she misses him. Ask straight-out is there something going on in his life? Listen attentively and wait for a response.

Example 2: Assuming is One's Responsibility

At work, a co-worker showed Angel her daughter's hand knitted tams. She asked if she would like her daughter to knit her one.

Angel replied, "Sure."

Imagine her surprise when she was charged $10.00. Angel thought the tam was going to be a gift—she felt exploited. Somehow in our busy lives, it is easy to assume. We have to take responsibility for our assumptions.

Example 3: Assuming and Expectation

Let us pretend Roberta was having a Halloween costume party for her birthday. You offered to make her outfit as a birthday gift. You also made her mother's costume, for which you were amply paid.

Down the line, Roberta asked you to make her son's costume. You told her you would love to. While you were paying for the Roberta's pattern and material, Roberta placed her son's material and pattern with your order.

You made her son's costume, but through each fitting, you felt aggravated and manipulated. You tried to approach the matter—the cost of the supplies, and the time it took to make the costume—except the tempo seemed off.

The day of the party you delivered the costumes. When you saw Roberta paying the caterer and DJ, you felt the same irritation swell in your stomach. It ruined the evening. You cannot believe your friend never offered to pay for her son's supplies and costume.

It is true, Roberta should have paid for her son's costume, but you have to take some of the responsibility. You never brought the expenses to her attention. Misunderstandings happen with expectations and assumptions—especially when there is money involved. If in doubt about anything, take an honest approach with a clear question. It is less harmful than waiting and later wishing you did.

Example 4: Assuming and Relationships

A woman whose husband passed away six months ago started emailing a childhood friend. Their emailing escalated to flirting. After a few months, they agreed to meet at his cabin. She lives miles away and he flew her to the location.

The meeting turned out to be a disaster. He was far from warm and fuzzy. In short, he was verbally abusive. He wanted what he wanted. They had a huge blow-up. He later drove her to a hotel and left her on her own.

Obviously, both parties had assumptions about the relationship. His agenda was to have someone by his side on his terms. She craved attention—probably romantically. She has to take responsibility for the mess she was in. She allowed herself to become passively engaged in a destructive relationship. Even if she did not fully process the grief from her loss, she still had an obligation to make a choice that kept her in a balanced place.

Example 5: Assuming and Speculating

Jean's marriage has been on the rocks for three months. She secretly felt all men were worthless. After having another argument with her husband, she slammed the door, and drove around town for an hour. Later she took herself out to lunch.

While she was having lunch, Jean happened to see her girlfriend's husband with a female neighbor in a far corner of the restaurant. As far as Jean was concerned, the couple looked like they were cozying up to each other. She was sure they were having an intimate conversation. Jean angrily thought to herself, I should tell Mara I saw her husband lunching with the pretty neighbor.

Jean is living in her head. How can she be fully aware of the situation concerning her neighbors? If Jean decides to speak to Mara without weighing the facts, it would be a malicious act. There is a saying by Ben Franklin that I often repeat to myself. "Believe none of what you hear and half of what you see."

Not everything is what it seems to be. Maybe if Jean was thinking clearly instead of assuming, she could have stopped by the table and said hello to her neighbor and her friend's husband. Speculating about a situation does not serve a purpose. Jean is responsible for her actions and how her actions affect her friend. Note that what one feels is for him or her. What one does affects everyone else.

NERVOUSNESS AND FEAR

Nervousness is a strong sensation, usually fear based. This natural mechanism helps us to be concerned about something that could cause us bodily harm—a threat. When people try to ignore their nervousness, they become immobilized.

Examine your patterns of nervousness. Do you find new or out-of-the-ordinary circumstances trigger your nervous system? When you are nervous or fearful are you unreasonable or illogical in your thinking? If so, try practicing meditation techniques (see Chapter XIX, Meditation and Space).

Fear/depression: An abnormal or unpleasant emotion, a dread, apprehension, or a misgiving. I do not know of anyone who has not experienced some form of fear/depression at least once in a life time. In this state, it is difficult to go outside oneself, it cripples one's growth to move forward, and one feels miserably trapped. By changing what one fears into a challenge, there is a good chance the quality of one's life will bloom, or at least, one will find some relief.

If fear/depression escalates beyond reason, seek professional help. Nowadays there are medications that could relieve some of the symptoms of this immobilizing experience.

CHAPTER V

*The answer to your question resides in
nature's infused energy.*

AWARENESS

Awareness is digested through our senses and shifts our perception. But once we allow our memory—a trigger reaction—to corrupt our awareness we lose our energy flow. Observe how you feel when an illusion becomes dismantled. In that intense moment, you may feel that you have lost your identity—as though you have stepped out of yourself. Trust the action of awareness and grasp your reality—where everything falls into place.

Through awareness, you will find a simple stillness. There are no bombarding thoughts. The YOU is empty and your words flow. You empathically sense another person's reality and realize his or her reality is important. This clarity gives you freedom from your illusions—perceived ideas. As your heart opens, you experience an airiness and your ego will cease to have power.

Example: Awareness

A woman met a man online. They communicated online and by telephone. When they first began to email, he mentioned he did not have a girlfriend. After relating every day for two months, she mentioned she would like to visit him. He confessed he had a girlfriend and added he was under house arrest.

She told him under the circumstances she would rather remain friends. She did not want him thinking they were going to be an item someday. A few weeks ago he said flat out, "I know you want me and I want you, so let us just move forward.

She said, "No."

Now she is wavering. She told me he seems like such a nice person and she wants to give him a chance. The woman in this story is not aware of the road she is embarking on. The fact that she is even contemplating further contact with this guy should force her to have her head examined. This man is a liar. He is under house arrest. And he is far from being a nice person.

It is obvious she does not have a high opinion of herself. I suggested she seek counseling. Sugarcoating a foolish situation like this could be potentially dangerous. And her actions should be addressed.

INSIGHT

Insight is of an inner nature relating to specific events that move us toward pertinent information. It is an inborn tool that guides us to do the right thing—nature's way of opening our experiences. It creates a knowing (an understanding) without focusing on conscious reasoning. The preciseness of intuition depends on how much you care for yourself and how much you see yourself as part of another person.

Insight cannot be forced or coaxed; it takes a special kind of focusing to be part of this trouble-free zone. One must be careful not to cloud an insight with anticipation or expectations. Allow this silent place to flow into an unexplored area—an "aha" moment—where you will comprehend a deeper understanding to a situation and find it easier to live in the present moment, thus experiencing less uncertainty.

Be assured, it only takes a small amount of information to spark your insights. Once you have experienced the unvarnished truth you stop mulling over situations and your wavering doubts lift. I am not speaking of normal doubts, the kind of doubt one experiences just before making a decision. I mean the haunting fearful doubts; the doubts that keep you stuck—truth cannot cause doubt.

If you find yourself rationalizing information, you are not experiencing insight. Watch how your mind drags you back into the past to rehash an experience or an old idea. Do not allow your ego to malign your insights (see Chapter XVII, "Life's Wake-Up Call" and "Destiny's Deliverance").

INTUITION, KNOWING, AND NOT KNOWING

With a knowing you have a keen discernment and astuteness. There is a safe silence, an openness, and a willingness to accept an answer. How do you know you are receiving a knowing answer versus an answer based on your ego? A knowing moment is void of space and time. The experience is alive and fresh with a freeing movement. It is a driven force and does not hold itself back.

If you are uncomfortable or worry about making a mistake, you will never have a knowing. A knowing may not always make sense, but if you wait, time will prove your knowing was correct. A knowing decision has nothing to do with friends, family, or opinions. You are the keeper of the knowing moment. It is a private experience; it is right for you. A knowing is part of a normal human experience. Never allow someone else's criticisms to diminish what you know.

Example 1: Knowing and a Surprise

Beth's Aunt Valerie passed away and bequeathed an heirloom broach to her cousin Sandra. On Beth's birthday, Sandra gave Beth the broach. Beth felt embarrassed accepting the broach—it was significantly valuable. Shyly she suggested Sandra should sell the broach.

Sandra made it clear to Beth she would never think of selling the broach since it meant so much to her aunt. And she truly wanted her to have it. Sandra told Beth every moment she saw her wearing the broach she would think of Aunt Valerie.

Beth felt overwhelmed by Sandra's generosity. A secret part of her thought she would be indebted to Sandra forever. Yet she could feel Sandra's sincerity. Beth took a deep breath. She searched within without preconceiving an idea or thought—suddenly she had a knowing.

She said, "Thank you, Sandra, for the gracious gift. I will always treasure the broach, but mostly your thoughtfulness."

This new experience will add a deep dimension to both Beth's and Sandra relationship.

Example 2: Knowing, Dismissing Uncomfortable Feelings

Let us suppose a person named Mike is having difficulties with his living arrangements. You volunteer to help and invited him to move into your apartment—temporarily—until he is able to find permanent lodgings. Before Mike becomes part of your household you mention he has to pay for his half of the utilities and purchase his food.

When the utility bills arrived, Mike was not receptive. He told you he could not afford to pay his share. You firmly explained you do not have the means to support him. He insists he will borrow the money from his friend Carol. The next day, Mike explains that Carol will give him the money by the end of the week. He begs you to be patient.

He looks you square in the eye with sincerity. He said, "You will receive your money."

Your knowing tells you Mike is not being forthright. But you decide to dismiss your feelings and give into Mike's request. Unfortunately, in the middle of the week—while you were at work—Mike stole your jewelry, ipod, DVD, and television set.

Some people are moochers. They are not anyone's friends. Being kind and generous is fulfilling, but one has to be cautious. Before you allow someone into your home, make sure he or she can be trusted. I find when the red flag feeling presents itself there is always more to a story than initially presented. Listen to your spirit and consider your knowing as a warning sign. Do your best not to become a victim.

Example 3: Knowing, Ignoring the Alarm

I heard this example from a friend. A man and a woman met on an Internet dating site. Very quickly the relationship bloomed. The man quit his seven year engineering job and followed his new love to another state. After a few weeks of living together he pressured her into marrying him. Something in her heart told her they were moving too quickly. But even though she felt uncomfortable, she married him anyway.

Four months into their marriage she knew she made a mistake. He has cheated on her, he does not have a job, and—on top of that—he has bad credit. She wants out of the marriage. He is trying to emotionally blackmail her into giving him half the worth of her home or else he will contest the divorce.

This woman bears the responsibility for entering into a union before she had enough information to make a clear decision. It is time she save herself before she loses more ground. In this critical situation, I suggested she call a lawyer and ask about her rights.

Example 3: Not Knowing, Too Trusting

In a grocery store line, two friends had an intense conversation. One friend mentioned he was robbed. He said since it was the summer time, he thought it would be fun to entertain his business colleagues on his boat. Before anyone boarded, he placed his grandfather's antique Rolex watch on his bedroom nightstand. Needless to say, someone took his watch—it is irreplaceable. He said he could not image who could have taken it. He trusted everyone.

Again, if anyone has a group of people in their home or otherwise, they should display caution. Sometimes, under the right circumstance, people will do things out of character. Why take the chance—be prepared.

Example 4: Not Knowing, Camouflaging Emotions

I heard a story many years ago that went something like this. A young child notices a wounded poisonous snake lying on the ground. The snake pleads with her; help me get my health back to normal.

The child said, "Will you bite me when you recover from your injury?"

The snake quickly replied, "Of course not, I appreciate you caring for me."

The child showed her friends the beautiful snake. They could not believe how kind he was and how readily he played with them.

One day the snake told the child he had recovered from his wounds. He was homesick and he wanted her to take him into the deep forest. The child agreed to help him. She reminded him he was not to bite her.

Throughout the journey the child walked anxiously into the deep forest. Abruptly, the snake asked the child to stop—he was home. As the child started to place the snake on the ground, he bit her hand. The child screamed in pain. She anticipated her sure death.

Sobbing she asked the snake, "Why after all I have done for you did you renege on your promise?"

The snake simply answered, "I am what I am."

Only through living in the present can one understand the circumstances in one's surroundings. Note every time you are in a precarious situation—use scrutiny. Always consider the source. Some people play on one's sympathies to camouflage their true motives. Anytime you are helping someone because you feel sorry for him or her that is not a knowing.

WISDOM

Wisdom is a way of life where courage and confidentiality prevail. It does not allow anyone to sidestep an uncomfortable situation or expect applause or admiration. Wise people usually do not become frantic about their upheavals. They are flexible under the most outrageous circumstances. Yes, they may feel bewildered by life's disappointments or an unforeseen tragedy, but they usually keep their wits about them. They prepare for the unexpected and make a conscious effort to let go of their dogmatic tendencies.

Wise people know they are responsible for their own lives. They do not blame others for their hardships. They practice clarity. They balance their lives with love and kindness.

They are good listeners. Best yet, they always react to someone else's opinion with respect. They do not waste time looking for sunshine on a rainy day. They reflect sunshine—their glow shines from within. They serendipitously travel on that path of the unexpected. They live in the relationship of knowing they are the teacher and the pupil.

Can you evolve to be a wise person? Sure, by following a few simple rules anyone can become a wise person.

• Manage your actions to the best of your ability.
• Question the tenets of your foundation.
• Don't create by chance; create by choice.
• Hold out for the best.
• You can make amazing things happen through meditation. Concentrate on the colors of a rainbow, smell the grass, or focus on the height of the sky.
• Have the gumption to use your voice, even when you feel fearful.

•There are many styles at delivering the truth, and yours is important.

•Establish what is worth fighting for before you jump into ring.

MAKE A DECISION

There is real power being able to both observe yourself and be yourself at once. That is when you become a stronger, smarter, and proactive. Let your decisions be based on wisdom rather than raw emotions. And if you happen to experience a setback, down the line you may find it was not a setback after all. Solve your problems simply. The answer is always hidden within a dilemma.

For example: Going out to dinner with a group and their preferences can be unsatisfying. To eliminate this problem, here are a few suggestions.

• When the majority of the group wants something a certain way or someone tries to strong-arm you in making a certain decision—assert yourself. You have a voice.

• If you are at a restaurant and you do not want to pay as part of a group, ask for a separate check.

• If you are a vegetarian and others want to have a meal where meat is served—you have a right to graciously excuse yourself.

CHAPTER VI

Indulge someone you love or a person who loves you.

COMPASSION

Compassion is giving of oneself while you metaphorically join with another—recognizing the pain of a person's suffering. At this interval, you bring awareness into someone's life and give him or her new levels of understanding. The act of compassion wears many faces. Try smiling or stating a please or thank you, often. You will find that these small gestures ensure a healthy heartfelt connection.

Example 1: Compassion in the Subway

After three consecutive stops, the subway cars did not have any seats available. At the fourth stop, a pregnant woman entered the car. Everyone was tightly squeezed together. She looked pleadingly at several passengers hoping someone would relinquish a seat. Automatically the passengers shifted their eyes away from her stare. A few minutes later, a middle-aged man noticed the woman's discomfort. He motioned for her to take his seat.

Example 2: Compassion Toward a High School Friend

Paul is haunted by his unstable family life. He has been shuffled back and forth from his mother's home to foster homes since he can remember. When he was a high school senior, his mother flew to Arizona to visit an ex-boyfriend. She never returned.

Tony, Paul's best friend, asked his parents if Paul could stay with them. Tony's family felt compassion for Paul. During the family conference, Tony's parents explained to Paul they expected him to attend school daily and keep his grade average to a B. If he did not do as they asked, he would be placed with the state's child welfare department.

Paul was grateful. He felt fortunate he would be able to attend school and receive a high school diploma with the rest of his classmates. Paul thanked Tony's parents and agreed to their terms.

Periodically through the next few months, Tony's mother asked Paul questions about school and his homework. Paul told her he was focused. Four months from the time Paul moved into Tony's home, his mother came home from work early. She caught Paul playing a video game on the computer. She immediately called his school. Unknown to her, Paul had been playing hooky for the past two days. She was very upset; Paul had broken her trust.

Tony's parents told Paul, they would give him one chance to prove himself. Faithfully, Paul attended school for a month, until one sunny spring day he slid into a lazy mode. He decided to stay home from school and justified his action by thinking he would work on his science project.

When Tony came home from school, he was shocked. He could not believe Paul skipped school again. He tried to tell him that his parents were serious, and he had better straighten out.

He said, "My Dad meant what he said. He will send you to the state's child welfare department." Paul chose to ignore Tony's voice of reason.

Sporadically, for weeks, Paul would get up in the morning have breakfast with the family, and later do as he pleased. The day of reckoning came when Tony's father accidentally saw Paul at the community mall. Paul tried to make a legitimate excuse to Tony's father, but he was not having any of it.

He said, "Paul I am not happy to see you here. You know the rule. Come home with me. You are packing your bags. I have finished trying to help you."

The authorities intervened. Tony's parents opened their home and showed Paul compassion—Paul did not reciprocate. He made a choice by following a pattern of deception and unreliability. He did not understand that Tony's parents were giving him empowerment over his dreary situation. It takes both parties to open their energy field and to make a commitment.

Example: Not Compassionate
When people feel entitled, they treat others shabbily in order to boost their ego—to feel superior. This act is the opposite of compassion. A friend of mine told me this story. His brother's daughter put herself through college and medical school; she was the first in her family to graduate from college. His niece furthered her education and later had other initials after her M.D.

At a family gathering, she bragged about her knowledge and her superior intellect. In front of several people, she told her first cousin she would be making a six figure salary, and since her cousin is a clerk in a department store her life would never amount to anything. Her cousin was hurt and left the dinner table without speaking. Her uncle tried to explain his niece her derogatory remarks was unacceptable behavior. The young doctor could not understand what all the fuss was about. She refused to apologize.

More recently, she has been reprimanded for making insulting remarks to her co-workers. Some people are destined to learn life's lessons the hard way. Being mean-spirited will never bring joy into anyone's life. And acting in this manner confirms it.

SHARING AND COMPASSION

What is the difference between the act of compassion and sharing? Compassion has an all-embracing understanding of an individual and their circumstance. Sharing is contributing something physically such as volunteering one's time—sharing is tangible.

Example: Sharing

While Bill and Sara were waiting at the doctor's office, she found a candy bar at the bottom of her purse. Bill broke-out in a colossal smile. He exclaims to Sara, excitedly, her candy bar is his favorite.

Effortlessly, Sara broke the candy bar in two pieces, and gave half to Bill. She did not think how kind she is, or how lucky Bill should feel. Nor did Sara look back wishing she kept the candy bar for herself.

Exercise:

For a month look at the following sharing examples. Remember sharing has nothing to do with feeling sorry for someone. Moreover, when we are truly sharing, one does not have the attitude he or she is owed a favor in return.

Examples

- Share your time, such as taking someone on an errand.
- Prepare a special dinner
- Present a gift (the value is insignificant).
- Call someone who would like to hear your voice.
- Give someone your undivided attention—the most priceless gift of all.

KINDNESS

The act of kindness speaks from one's innate spirit. It is a forward motion that shows a sensitive, unstrained freedom. People who are willing to risk rejection and freely open themselves (their harmonic vibration) are special individuals. They understand the gift of sharing and do not feel inconvenienced when they go out of their way for someone.

Example: Kindness

Ashley was walking through the neighborhood when she saw a puppy in distress. He was aimlessly running in the street. She grabbed and petted him to calm him down. After he relaxed, she tied her belt around his collar. She walked through the neighborhood and asked neighbors if they knew where the dog belonged. Needless-to-say, the owners appreciated Ashley's act of kindness.

SENSITIVITY

Being sensitive shows you know how to react to a situation that may be either awkward or controversial. When one is unbiased, the right words fall into place. If in doubt, it is best to say nothing at all—just listen.

Example: Sensitivity

Let us suppose a married friend told you she wants to leave her husband for a man she has befriended at work. She explains they have so much in common and, best yet, he is her ideal man. Whenever she is with him she feels free.

By coincidence, you happen to know this man is a womanizer; he has had at least two office flings. You realize if you tell her the blatant truth you would crush your friend's heart. Also, there is a strong possibility she may not believe you.

In a gentle persuading voice, ask her to wait before making such a drastic decision. Maybe it is time to search within, take a breather, and step away from her co-worker for a week or so. You guide her to seek marital counseling. Besides, seeing a therapist may help her learn something about herself.

You also ask her to retrace her steps and question how she arrived at this place. What are the issues she is having with her husband? Does her co-worker/lover actually possess the qualities she thinks he has? After you have said your piece, let it go. The end results are in her hands.

WHAT DOES A FAVOR MEAN TO YOU?

There are people who award favors, and then wait anxiously for someone to return the favor. This person does not live in the moment. People who have this attitude cannot enjoy a true relationship with anyone; their lives are contradictory.

Example: Favor

Let us suppose your children and the neighbor's child attend the same private school. One afternoon your neighbor asked you to pick up her son while you were retrieving your three children. For the next three Tuesdays you picked up the neighbor's son from school.

The fourth week your car required extensive repairs. It was going to be out of commission for two days. You asked your neighbor to bring your children to and from school for a week.

To your surprise, she said, "No."

She explained she was going away on business trip, and her mother would be taking care of her son. She mentioned that her mother was not well enough to be responsible for three extra children. Now you are in a snit. You feel your neighbor should be obligated to help; after all, you have been doing her a favor for weeks.

Ask yourself this question. Were you being generous because you unconsciously wanted a favor in return? Generosity, for its own sake brings joy. When you have clarity with your intentions, there is no jealously, revenge, or conflict.

The past is gone. Start a new relationship with your neighbor with a heartfelt dialogue. Possibly, you could make other arrangements for future unforeseen circumstances.

Questions:

Do you feel you go out of your way to accommodate everyone, but no one returns your favor? Are you capable of sharing in another person's interest? Have you shown kindness toward a stranger—lately?

•Deepen your awareness by opening your harmonic energy field.

CHAPTER VII

Love comforts the magic hidden in the human heart.

WHAT LOVE IS NOT

Within all humans, there dwells a powerful force of an instinctual nature to reach out and touch and be touched by someone. We want this so passionately, emotionally, and physically we are easily led in the wrong direction.

There are movies, songs, and all types of sonnets that express the joys and torment associated with falling in love. And it is ironic how many of us have love in our lives, but we knead and pull at it like a wad of dough until it no longer resembles the love we once enjoyed. Let us question "what love is and what love is not." In the examples below, find what the word love means to you.

Example: Love, Infatuation

When I was a teenager, I worked in the housekeeping department at the Lying-In-Hospital in Providence, Rhode Island (presently called Women and Infants). I had a tremendous crush on a college student. Secretly, I called him Blue Eyes. I thought of him every minute. When I saw him, I would float on air. For one year, I kept my secret passion to myself until Sharon, a co-worker, noticed me staring at Bradley. She cleverly confronted me and I was too naïve to resist chiming my story.

About a month later, Bradley, asked me to go to a movie. I could feel my face turn red and I literally thought I was going to explode. I stuttered and mumbled something. When he asked me to repeat what I had said. I could not speak. It seemed as though my throat was in a winch. I forced myself to look into his wonderful blue eyes. His smile told me he was enjoying my plight. In that moment, I knew Sharon told him I liked him.

I took a deep breath and told him no. He was not happy. To my surprise, he tried to bully me into going out with him. I smiled and told him I appreciated the invite, but my parents would not allow me date him since he was much older. I told him my age. His face softened and I could tell my statement saved him from embarrassment.

At one time, I thought if I was ever going to fall in love it would be with Bradley. But after being confronted with the real Bradley, I lost the dreamy fascination of him. Although, the truth be told, every time I looked into his blue eyes, a part of me still melted.

LOVE IS NOT A PHYSICAL ATTRACTION

How many people readily express they will not form a relationship with someone unless he or she feels that special butterfly quiver? The butterfly quiver has nothing to do with one's character or compatibility. In all probability, it is a physical chemistry—a beginning—but by no means a promise to an end.

Take a minute and ask your spirit if the person in your life is right for you. Behold an individual's personality and ethical differences with clarity. Relationship progression is built with understanding and compromise. It is a slow grow-on-you-as-you-go process.

Some people think they are being independent by allowing themselves to invest in a purely physical relationship. Yes, like so many quick fixes there is a release from that pent-up alone feeling. For many busy people, it is easier to have quick physical encounters than to concentrate on the fine qualities of a relationship.

In truth, our relationships—no matter how shallow or deep—are the mirror of the dimensions within us. When we suppress our need to relate, we also repress those dimensions. Temporary outcomes, especially made in the bedroom, do not change people's lives or give them full hearts.

Example: Love, Dangerous and Exciting

A friend of mine continually derails her stable relationships. She runs off with someone who tends to cheat, lie, and—in some cases—steal from her. Inevitably, she terminates the drama; finds someone decent, and then begins her downward cycle again.

There is something in her that craves an adrenaline rush. She finds the dangerous types and unstable men lacking an emotional intensity, but she likes how they keep her guessing. She never knows when she is going to fall off the tightrope from a thrill or crash from a rejection.

She's clearly not thinking... or at least she's not thinking clearly. She's making emotional decisions rather than rational ones. No doubt she adores her dangerous man. But will she be able to trust him? Is that love? Her false thinking is an illusion.

Love Is Not Pretending

Manipulating a loved one to attain what you want is far from love. A true act of loving anyone is loving a person for who they are, and not for whom you wish them to be.

Example: Love, Self-Centeredness Shrouds Love

Throughout Doug's childhood his family treated him with indifference—most of the time he was left to shift for himself. At the age of eight, his parents divorced. Neither parent was dedicated to his well-being or mature enough to give him love. Their inaction made him feel neglected and lonely. He coped with his unhealthy environment by using his wit to divert attention from his insecurities.

Underneath all his bravado, Doug was a miserable, angry person. He secretly cursed everybody—thinking someone else's life was easier than his. He related to people as if he was watching a play—disconnected (see Chapter XV, Unfulfilled People).

Since he was never satisfied in his space, he would prey on people's weaknesses. He never cared what kind of destruction he caused. Anytime he was confronted with a ghastly deed, he made excuses to justify his behavior.

He rarely apologized, and when he did, he looked at the gesture as another form of perfecting his technique. Doug's self-centeredness depletes his energy field. Eventually, he will lose his sense of connection to his spirit and bitterly blame others for his empty life.

LOVE AND LIES

There are degrees of lying. Everyone has heard of the white lie—a lie to soften a hostile situation. And there is the dark lie—a lie to deceive or manipulate. I admit I have told my share of white lies in order to protect someone. Or I have omitted the truth about something because it would have done no one any good to repeat what I knew.

Generally, I feel the truth will set one free. Lying reshuffles one's challenges, and they do not solve anything. Everyone has to make the call for oneself, and later own-up. In either case, anything that is concealed causes conflict.

Example: Love and Lying

Kelly has been married for ten years. She accidentally discovered her husband has been in contact with an ex-girlfriend; they were an item fifteen years earlier. The girl-friend broke it off.

When he was confronted, he explained he did not want to tell her because he would not want to know if she werein touch with an ex-boyfriend. She feels annoyed that he was not open with her.

Intimacy begins at home not outside the home. Partners should be transparent about their relationships with each other. And for the sake of their marriage, the missing details ought to be disclosed. I think it is best they have a deep conversation in the presence of a marriage counselor. I suggested her husband pick the analyst.

LOVE IS NOT AN ILLUSION

Below are the few examples that relate to love illusions:
- Love cannot diminish our demons from the past.
- Love will not make life easier or happier.

• Love cannot make Mr. or Ms Wrong into a Mr. or Ms Right.

• Never expect anyone to be "the one."

• Peek behind one's bravado and demeanor. Explore the hidden side of a person. Annoyances in the present moment are not going away.

• If one is providing for his or her family that does not mean one should dismiss other family necessities such as compassion and affection.

• When you think another person has to change to make your life perfect, you do not understand the art of loving.

• Some men and women are physically or emotionally abusive. They may apologize for their action or flamboyant indiscretion, yet think nothing of practicing the same negative habit again.

• When it comes to the matters of the heart, the person who says "no," for whatever reason, should be respected.

LOVE VERSUS REJECTION

I would like to address the heartache of loving someone who may not love you. Everyone will experience this disappointment throughout life—we adjust. Furthermore while someone is expressing their truth, even if it feels painful, deliberately avoiding it can produce the same results. When we truly love a person—and for our self-growth—we must allow that person who has rejected us to live in peace.

I feel sour love affairs should be broken off at the ankle. Do not contact an ex or attempt to persuade him or her to come back to you. If you do, you two will repeat the same dance until both of you have had enough.

Much of our misery has to do with an expectation or loss of a connection than it has to do with love. Let us compare love to a diamond and cubic zirconia. The zirconia may sparkle like a diamond—but it is not the real thing. It does not have the same depth. It is the same for love. If you are not thankful for the love you have felt, you have not experienced love—forgo your attachment.

Do not sit in judgment or feel a failed relationship was a lost opportunity. Someone else's opinion of us should not improve or disprove our image. And everyone has a right to be in a space that makes him or her feel full.

I find the pursuit of marriage proposals a burning issue with some couples. Listen to each other and clear the air how both of you feel about marriage. If the factor of marriage is not what one part of the couple wants, the relationship is bound to head toward a self-destructive path.

Example: Love, Regret, and Rejection

Let us suppose a friend of yours introduced you to a man named Vincent. From the beginning both of you enjoyed each others company. You fell hopelessly in love with him. On a weekend getaway, he suggested it was time to look at engagement rings. After several stores, you had cozy lunch at an outside restaurant.

Based on one of Vincent's commitments, you thought it was time to confront him about a personal subject you have been keeping on the back burner. He did not respond well to your conversation. A week later he dumped you without an explanation. You are still madly in love . Daily, you beat yourself-up thinking you should have delayed speaking with him until he gave you a ring.

Put yourself to the test. Ask "why" you took so long to address a personal issue in the first place? Would you want to live with someone who refuses to compromise or speak to you about uncomfortable situations? You cannot change anyone. You can only change yourself.

Start expressing how you feel. Be disconcerting and specific about what you want. This will attract people who genuinely like you for the person you are, and repel those who do not. I think it is better to take a stiff rejection in the beginning of a relationship than wait indefinitely for the "we need to have a serious talk."

Love Is An Action

Saying love is not showing love. Feeling love is not love. Love is a benevolent action. It is like throwing away part of ourselves to attain the new—a transformation. It is the ultimate opportunity in which we can give to each other while fulfilling one's individual completeness. Love is part of the wonder of what is. We are what we love.

Love cannot be measured or rushed. And it takes time to weave two unique realities together. Also, love cannot survive if one does not learn to manage to cap his or her debilitating egotistical emotions—separating one from the very person one loves. Fall into the abyss of loving—where there are no beginnings or endings. This is where you will feel alive and free.

Example 1: Love is Honoring the Connection

Harold's father passed away when he was seventeen. He joined the Army to educate himself and subsequently made the military his career. At the age of forty, he met the woman who became his wife and began a family in England. He made it a point to visit his mother and siblings in the United States every other year.

Two years before Harold's mother passed away, she told Harold's siblings she had sold property, settled stocks, and placed money in a special trust fund that they would receive upon her death. She mentioned since she rarely saw Harold and did not feel close to him she was leaving him out of her will. Harold's siblings tried to explain to their mother that Harold would be devastated. He did his best to visit her whenever he had the chance; she refused to listen.

Upon Harold's mother's death, his three siblings unanimously agreed they should divide their inheritance with Harold. They hired a lawyer and made Harold an equal partner. They cared for their brother, deeply. They also knew how much Harold loved his mother. Harold's siblings never mentioned he was disinherited.

Example 2: Love Does Not Mean You are Always Right

Mandy had an upsetting day. She sat back in her chair ramrod stiff. She tried to relax by pushing her fingers through her hair. She could not avoid the strange twinge she felt in her stomach. She had another run-in with her sister, Tonya. She thought, "What is wrong with people? Why are they so difficult and disappointing?"

She sighed in confusion. She felt she had paid her dues. She worked twenty-four hours a week for seven years while she put herself through college. She graduated with two masters degrees. It took her another three years before her career showed progress and another year after that to rise to a prestigious position. In the business world, she knows how to use her expertise—her confidence fills the air.

Mandy lumps everyone into one box. She quarrels over the smallest point. Forcibly, she maintains her stance. She treats everyone in her family as though she has a task to complete. And she immediately shows a haughty indignant quality whenever those close to her do not stroke her ego. She does not detect any difference between leading a group of co-workers to accomplish a task or to intimately relate to someone.

True dialogue is expressing oneself from the heart. Respecting each other brings a spontaneous understanding of one another's sacred space—agreeing to disagree: therefore, foregoing power struggles.

How To Love Yourself

You must love yourself before you can rightly love anyone else. Every day take a minute of your time to delve deeply into your psyche. In the morning, look in the mirror and give yourself an affirmation. For example: I like and love myself. I deserve the best my life has to offer.

Love yourself. Hug your spirit. Through this daily practice, you will find an elation that could never be met through any external means. It is an exploration—an ongoing one—to bring you to your higher self where contentment resides.

Do you notice how some people live a life of misery? It is not so much they are incapable of happiness as they are afraid of it. They complain to protect themselves from being let down. They do not speak from their heart. They live in a whirlpool of ignorance—afraid of their own voices. Somehow they think it is easier to have a defeatist attitude than be surprised by anything new. If one cannot love oneself, how can one truly love anyone else?

Learn To Love

The first lesson of love is to learn to love those who love you—even when you think a person is not personally special. Take a moment to feel the expression of love being shown—do not limit your inner circle. One cannot have too many individuals love him or her. Be grateful a person appreciates you.

I know an elderly lady who thinks of me as the daughter she never had. Her face lights-up every time we see each other. Even though I do not feel close to her, I will ask her about her day and comment on subjects where we have a common interest. I also give her a hug now and then—another way to honor our human connection.

A Choice: Love Or Fear

Feel your creativity. Do not waste your time wishing for something you think you want. It enforces more wanting—the ego is never satisfied. Do not live in your mind or get caught in the idea of rejecting or excluding a person because his or her ideas interfere with your way of thinking. Do not allow fear to guide your heart. Check yourself. Be cognitive of your actions. Always give gratitude for what you already have. If you are looking for guidance, have faith; a teacher will gently appear.

Exercise:

Talk to a dear friend. Tell your friend about your insecurities and fears. Ask your friend to describe his or her insecurities and fears. Laugh at yourselves. I doubt either one of you would want to walk in each other's shoes.

Questions:

How do you define love? Do you feel loved? Do you avoid intimacy? Do you secretly feel you love your loved one more than he or she loves you? Do you easily fall in love to feel less lonely? Are you willing to share another person's joy, sorrow or—best of all—discover another person's truth?

•Listen to your answers. This is the beginning of self understanding.

THE INNER CIRCLE

The people in our inner circle indirectly contribute to our daily existence. Therefore, we must be careful who we invite to be part of our inner circle. Question if they reflect light around you or do they subtly produce a dark cloud where you feel at odds with the present moment—unsettling you.

Question the stability of your relationship. Separate what is "your problem" from what is "their problem." If someone in your inner circle cannot listen to a viewpoint or show you common courtesy, speak up. It will not cause a ruckus to those who truly love you—they will unconditionally understand.

Questions:

Do you benefit from the people in your inner circle? Are they supportive? Do they help you rise to a higher spiritual level?

•Reacquaint yourself with those who live in your space, and then make a decision accordingly. This is a spiritual crossroad experience.

HIDDEN CHARACTERISTICS

There are six key hidden personal characteristics that show our individual nature: physical/action, verbal/expressive, affectionate/warm, sympathizer/compassionate, and cerebral/loner. People are either multitasking or slow as you go type. One layer is neither better nor worse than another. The primary layer is the strongest. The secondary layer is the modifier. It is like a bridge that links one characteristic to another.

In the beginning of all relationship, we touch upon all the six hidden characteristics. But as we become relaxed our true hidden characteristic emerges with a strong potency. This is where tensions build. For example—in a romantic situation—if two individuals' hidden character layers are completely different, one may feel a partner has changed or he or she is no longer in love. A parent may feel close to an infant or toddler, but as the child matures, a parent and child may feel estranged

When one's hidden characteristic blends with an individual, there is a comfortable bond that holds them together. If two individuals' hidden characteristics are opposite, there is conflict. This does not mean it is impossible to get along. It means one will have to compensate for the other's differences.

Note when a physical person is romantically involved with a verbal person tensions may rise. When a cerebral/loner person is romantically involved with an affectionate/warm person, the affectionate/warm person may feel unloved. Realize someone's hidden layer cannot change. It is who they are. Ask yourself, can you live with a person that is so very different than you?

I am a combination Sympathizer/Cerebral/Loner. I enjoy volunteering my time to help others. I give loved ones undivided attention, but I have a saturation level. Eventually, someone will have to wait until I replenish my energy. I need time to bask in my own space. I multitask.

My husband is a combination Cerebral/Loner/Physical. He also enjoys his space. He is a loner and home body. He enjoys reading and learning. He verbalizes when he is in the mood. He replenishes his energy by physical activities. His motto is slow-as-you-go. Note we have some traits in common—a connection.

I feel understanding the root of a loved one's hidden characteristic layer keeps a couple harmonized and contented. What is your hidden characteristic layers primary category?

Hidden Characteristic Identification Chart

• **Physical:** Playing sports, watching sports, enjoys all sorts of physical activities and outdoor activities, gym.

• **Verbal:** friendly, talkative and needs to express self often, may continually rehash a point.

• **Affectionate/Warm:** A touchy-feely type of person, needs attention and recognition, can be clingy, sometimes feelings are hurt easily.

• **Sympathizer:** Compassionate, a person who goes out of their way for others, they enjoy volunteering their time.

• **Cerebral/Loner:** Knowledge based, likes to read, may not express feeling well, needs space to recover from daily problems, may live in his or her head, may appear cold.

• **Multitasker:** Performs more than one duty at a time.

• **Slow-As-You-Go:** Like to stick to one subject before moving on to the next.

PART II
THE POWER OF UNDERSTANDING

THE EVENING ROSES

I see the roses
In the evening of their days
Blooming with magnificence
Yet ready to fade
They make me wonder
If we still have a chance
To make things right
To move to this blissful state
Where only life matters
Not the opinions that choke us
Into a silent mass

Bound by the depths of your heart
I throw away my thorns
Softly, I gather your name
Not to miss this hour
Mixed with roses
And the bloom
Hidden deep within me.

Chapter VIII

Know you are loved, even more than you think.

You and Your Universe

Before we can feel the magnitude of our spiritual life we must fulfill our primary physical necessities that are connected to the pragmatic world. It is essential we have food, shelter, warmth, and feel a sense of safety. Then we are able to aspire and meet our psychological needs. It is here we access another level of existence honoring our spirit—the true self; hereby we are ready to relate to others.

Our spirit is similar to the lantern's light. The light inside a kerosene lantern cannot shine through when the lantern's glass is clouded with grit. To allow our spirit's light to shine, one must honor his or her existence and recognize one's egotistical thinking—then we are able to show fellowship though compassion.

Our spirit's natural light radiates a magnificent glow by sharing what one knows and by bringing people together that otherwise would not have known one another. With each personal contact, we deepen our spiritual connection; we expand our world of love. Embrace these sacred moments, and finally, find the time to reflect on the day. These few simple side notes will help you open your spirit's essence.

MAJOR STAGES

Major stages lead us to behave and react in a certain manner. These stages are normal and healthy. As we enter the passage, we are thrown into two worlds—neither world is simple. The first major stage teaches us to understand facts. This is an important developmental phase—one wrestles with one's self-esteem. It is where we accept what is and who is good for us.

The second major stage acknowledges and resets terms as conditions change. We may wonder if we are walking in our right skin. It is a time to figure things out. A time to question what will make one feel better—or different.

Life's major stages give one a chance to build a fresh selfhood. Stay alert or in this poignant stage there is a strong chance you may make a life-long mistake or miss something you cannot grasp again. For example, teenagers as they approach adulthood begin to distance themselves from their parents. They have an impulse to play deaf. It is fairly normal for them to be moody and sulky. They no longer want to participate in family functions. They readily immerse themselves into new friendships, and begin to make choices—some with life long results.

For instance, I know several adults who left home as young teenagers to pursue a dream or run away from an empty home life. Let it be known one can never skip uncomfortable situations. These individuals are frozen in time—emotionally stunted. They did not learn how to cope with everyday situations or to make compromises.

I feel the ages between twelve and seventeen are important to one's mental and spiritual growth. The time slot (although precarious) graciously transforms a boy into manhood and a girl into womanhood. It adds to a child's emotional quotient (EQ) capacity. The child learns he or she is no longer an extension of a parent and becomes his or her own entity. This is the moment a child rises to a higher level of existence—a time of rebirth.

Similarly, middle-aged individuals may feel they have missed something profound in life. They may fantasize about finding a different partner, especially if their present relationship is challenging. They may look elsewhere to capture their youth. In this place, it is easy for them to romanticize relationships and decide to embark on an uncertain journey.

Mature individuals, unlike teenagers, are upfront about their feelings. They make it a point to interact with those closest to them. They are willing to share the complexities of their feelings.

Example: Major Stage, Behavior Problems

I know a seventeen-year-old who takes advantage of his parent's inability to follow through with punishments. He took the family car to a football game and later phoned his dad asking if he could stay overnight at his best friend's house.

His father told him "no" and he expected him home immediately. The next morning he nonchalantly strolled into his home. His blatant act of disobeying is nothing new. His parents had their usual "let us sit down and talk about your actions" conversation, but nothing has changed.

These parents are not doing their child a favor. They need to stop being a friend to their son and become responsible parents. A small effort on their part would make a difference in their son's behavior.

Nothing has an impact on a teenager as much as simply taking the car keys away for an allotted amount of time and having his dad or mom drive him to a destination. Yes, there will be tantrums and complaints, but this inconvenience will make an impact. Consequences should naturally flow from one's choices. What better time in life to learn this important lesson?

Questions:

Are you running to something or from something to distract or amuse yourself? Are you trying to keep your mind occupied, constantly? When you are at a loss, do you feel you are fulfilling a self-deserved prophecy? Are you having trouble going beyond a particular impasse?

* Realize everything is temporary. Step away from your funk by loving yourself and reach out to people who love you.

THE POWER OF THE INNER VOICE

Every individual ought to listen to his or her inner voice. According to one's conviction this voice could be God, Jesus Christ, angels, the higher self, the spirit within, or an extension of oneself. The inner voice exhibits wisdom and pursues love. If you ignore your inner voice you are bound to lead a marginal life.

You may ask how to distinguish the inner voice from your imagination or the ego's tempting messages. True guidance speaks to you in a nurturing command. Examples: Careful, a car is passing you on the right. You forgot your wallet on the kitchen table. Call your daughter, now. Slow down you are going too fast. Check your left tire. These messages make intuitive sense. They are positive and helpful.

In contrast, the ego has a mischievous sneakiness that drains one's sense of peace. The hollow monologue is disconnected. For instance: you are going to be late. Drive faster. Hurry! Pass that car. At the party, no one will like what you have to say. Note the disconnectedness. It is demeaning and makes one feel unsafe.

Example: The Ego Taking One Back to a Painful Place

Many of us have wondered if we should get back to an ex-boyfriend/girlfriend or renew an untrustworthy friendship. We are apt to remember the positive feelings and ignore the negative circumstances. Question facts: If there are no new facts available, trust the knowledge learned from the failed past—search within. The inner voice will lead you in the right direction. Making a mistake is always possible—lying to oneself all but guarantees it.

RELATING

Are you rough around the edges? Do you feel annoyed when others receive recognition instead of you? Are you a person who constantly wishes the position you are in could or should be different? Is your life more about wishing than doing?

If you are answering yes to one of these questions, take a step back. Find the distinction between your perception and the peace equated with silence. Note when you do appreciate something, you are not relying on your ego to make a validation. Allow life's universal energy (the connection) to enhance your insight and brighten your days.

Be brave enough to have a conversation about specific things in all relationships. Do not misrepresent yourself—honesty counts. There is no need to judge or presuppose an end result. Through relating and by practicing understanding one's character strengthens. Try this rule of thumb: It is not what one wants. It is not what the other wants, but a melting into the middle for what both of you want. This space is lined with peace.

Example 1: Relationship Compatibility
Mary Joe's girlfriend, Chrissie, is a fun person. She always has an idea to do something out of the ordinary. Sometimes she does things that are on the edge, a place where Mary Joe would not normally go. Two months ago they were almost arrested. Luckily, the arresting officer knew Mary Joe's father. He gave them a strong warning.

After being almost arrested, Mary Joe realized she is putting herself at risk. Going along with Chrissie's shenanigans will not be worth her ruining the rest of her life.

Example 2: Relationships Change
Marjorie and Art moved next door to Heather and Jeremy. They became the best of friends. They raised their children and took family vacations together. For thirty years, the two couples were almost inseparable. Suddenly, two months ago Jeremy passed away. Now, Heather no longer visits Marjorie and Art.

Heather needs to go through a grieving period. When Marjorie feels the time is right, she should visit Heather without Art. Have a heart to heart talk with her. Make it clear she is welcome to share in their lives. Add when Heather feels better she would like Heather to go on a trip with them. There is nothing like great friends and loving people to bring one to a better place.

FRIENDS

Friends in our lives are just as important as a partner—sometimes more so. As with all relationships, they should be intensely scrutinized. True relationships are not based on fantasy. Do not cling to any relationships that are detrimental to your spirit. Screen "what is" carefully. Note that, like the phases of the moon, relationships will wax and wane. Sometimes they burn brightly, illuminating our world—a time to enjoy. And at other times, they simply burn out—a time to move on.

Individuals often ask me this question. Is it possible for a single woman and a married man to remain friends or visa versa? I think it is highly possible to be "just friends." One guideline to follow: do not keep a loved one out of the loop—no secrets

Questions:

Is your attraction to certain individuals a recipe for unhappiness or dissatisfaction? Are your relationships filled with drama? Are you in a relationship that makes you feel numb?

• If you know—in your heart—there are underling problems in your relationships, stay attentive. Those problems will not go away.

Example: Friendship, Just Friends

My brother told me this story about his friend's wife, Claudia. By coincidence, Claudia met an old high school boyfriend while visiting her hometown. They had not seen each other in twenty-five years. Later they contacted each other online and agreed when she was in town visiting her aunt they would meet for lunch, have a drink, and share old photos. Claudia told her husband about meeting her friend, but neglected to mention they were planning to get together in three weeks.

When her husband found out about the meeting, he went off the deep end. He felt they were having a clandestine meeting. The arguing escalated. Claudia felt her husband was being unreasonable and was overreacting. She told him she just never got around to talking about the meeting. They came to an impasse. Consequently, her husband left their home and went to a hotel to cool off for three days.

One needs to place oneself in another person's shoes. While the husband may have been overreacting, he was the one who had to deal with the fact his wife was meeting a former friend/lover behind his back. At this point, any explanations will seem weak. For the sake of the marriage, it is best to apologize, beg for forgiveness, and terminate relating to the friend.

The most pure intention cannot make results happen. Claudia's husband deserves undivided attention and an assurance she will never go behind his back again.

Chapter IX

Listening is your healing power.

Family Issues

Expect that there will be one family member whose behavior does not play well with others. He or she tends to wreak havoc whenever the mood strikes by fueling the fire of misunderstanding. Always try to state a concern without being defensive. By offering a gentle opinion to a volatile situation or giving someone a pat on the back goes a long way. Place yourself in a state of grace. Do not expect someone to acknowledge you—sometimes it just does not come. The only time to protest loudly is when you feel someone's agenda (ego) is harming another person.

Realize you cannot make someone listen or understand you. However it is best to exhaust all means of making peace before declaring war. Ask yourself, in good conscience, have you done that? Depending on each other's dialogue, you can reach out or make it clear why you will not make peace.

Strive to move to a better place even if you have to cut your losses. Do not allow regret or misplaced judgments to get you down. Make an effort to stop worrying. Appreciate what is and continue to share yourself with others. Never close doors—unless completely necessary.

My husband and I went to a play that demonstrated the bitterness behind opinions. The mother was an atheist. She devalued the belief in a God and religion. Her son planned on becoming an Episcopal priest. The family was torn apart. When the son died unexpectedly, the mother realized her son had a right to live his life as he saw fit. And she wasted life's precious moments by feuding with her son about his life choices.

How many of us would do anything for our children, yet we personally allow our ego to speak from our hearts at the price of sacrificing all that is truly dear to us. Do not cut the quality of your relationships in half. Now is the time to take your ego out of all situations. The examples below will give more thoughts on the subject.

Example 1: Family Issues, People Change

Leslie has been married to Richard for seven years. Her son, Carl, at sixteen, was a handful. As a youngster, he was disrespectful and a terror. Moving forward, Carl has matured into a caring man. To Leslie's dismay, no matter how helpful Carl is to Richard, Richard never thanks or appreciates him. He continually brings up the past and he makes it clear he has no use for Carl.

When a woman brings her children into a marriage, technically speaking, the new husband is marrying her children—a co-parenting adventure. Richard and Carl may not like each other, but they should be respectful. For his own sake, Richard needs to demonstrate adult qualities and show forgiveness.

Sometimes we allow our past mistakes to take charge of our lives. And holding a grudge is one way to keep an unhappy event alive. By clinging to old memories, Richard is closing the door to the present moment and the future. Under these circumstances, a counselor may help the family to adjust to a new way of thinking.

Example 2: Family Issues, Feeling Superior
Jolene has a flannel-mouth. She nitpicks at her family's choices. She finds fault with a hair style, a choice of clothing, how to save or spend money, and the list goes on. The other day her sisters told her she was annoying them with her prejudicial remarks. Jolene became defensive. She feels she is helping.

Indirectly, Jolene is seeking approval—ego based. She enjoys spinning situations so her sisters will notice her. One cannot prevent Jolene from judging anyone. She probably does not "get it" and I doubt she will ever pat her sisters on the back and say, "Hey, that was a great idea."

They need to stop reacting and dancing to her tune. Make it clear she is crossing their boundaries. And if she does not have anything positive to say, they would rather she say nothing at all. No one appreciates a meddlesome person. In reality, unsolicited, impulsive antidotes are far from helpful. They only trigger mayhem.

Example 3: Family Issues, Wedding Date
My daughter's friend has been dating her fiancé for five years. When they finally set their wedding date, her fiancé's sisters were miffed. They asked them to change their wedding date since they were planning their wedding in the

same year and in the same summer months. They continually pressured them to reconsider their wedding date for the following winter. They have already placed a downpayment on a home, and they do not want to put their wedding off.

I think this young lady should hold her ground, but on the other hand, provoking new sisters-in-law may be a luxury she cannot afford. I suggested she plan her wedding in the earlier part of the spring. Besides, bumping her vows ahead of others proves she is a take charge type of woman. On a footnote, this incident may be an indication of future in-law dynamics. She should prepare herself for other unforeseen family opinions.

Example 4: Family Issues, Estranged Sister
Gertrude comes from a large family—seven sisters. She has been estranged from them since her parents passed away. She complains they never call or visit, but she knows they converse among themselves. She feels left out and annoyed. She comments they only speak with her when they want something. Gertrude should be open to learning about how she may have contributed to her problem and examine her behavior.

To make a fresh start, Gertrude could arrange a family conference. It is hoped that she will not seesaw back and forth about who is right or wrong or place blame. If necessary, she could apologize. This effort is bound to make headway. Everyone needs to learn to see each other as adults not as siblings struggling to receive mom's undivided attention. If her siblings cannot reciprocate, Gertrude has done her best, and then she can move on.

Example 5: Family Issues, Mother and Children

I heard a story from a woman whose mother is in an unstable situation. She married a manipulative man and he puts her adult children in a negative light. He spends money on himself, yet her mother has to ask permission to buy groceries, and later show her husband the register receipt.

Mom has left her husband several times, but manages to go back to him—again to repeat the same cycle of drudgery and complaints. Her daughters wish they could make her come to her senses. They plan on giving their mother an ultimatum. Choose to leave her husband or never see her daughters again. One cannot make anyone choose between two choices or else. It just does not work.

Reach out to mom. Ask her if there is anything they can do to help her. Explain to how they feel about her husband and the reasons why. Tell her they love her and enjoy spending time with her, but her volatile relationship is draining them.

Although it can be heartbreaking, their mom has to live her own life, and that means making choices and mistakes. Keep the lines of communication open. Urge mom to seek a counselor. Give her time to think. The decision is hers to make.

Example 6: Family Issues, Rejecting Negative Family Members

I know several women who were sexually abused as children—each by relatives. The perpetrators served jail time. As recovering adults, they refuse to associate or be in the presence of their abuser—family gatherings and weddings etc. Many relatives feel that the victims' estrangement makes life difficult on them.

Severe family problems act like a virus, infecting each person in a different way. Because families come in all shapes and configurations a person has a right to reject a relationship with his or her family member. One's sense of balance and emotional health cannot be compromised by others wishing a problem would go away. The person refusing to attend is wisely protecting him- or herself.

Example 7: Family Issues and Speaking Up

A woman married a middle-aged man who was divorced with two children. His new bride felt intimidated because his parents still displayed the old wedding pictures of his first wife and photos of the children with their mother. Her in-laws do not have one picture of their son with his new bride.

I suggested the couple make new pictures for the parents to hang in the home. A family portrait with his children would be nice. This gesture should ease the bride's insecurities.

Example 8: Family Issues, Tedious Relatives

Some elderly parents or grandparents can get stuck in a reminiscing mode. They may treat their relatives like an audience and fuel a conversation with a one-sided version of ancient history or family gossip. I think it is up to each individual to shape the direction of their conversations.

Decide what you have in common, and engage in the subject wholeheartedly. Ask about certain significant experiences. If someone gets side-tracked with gossip, change the direction. Play cards and look at family photographs. Nothing makes a day go by faster than being creative and sharing a listening ear.

The elderly have a lot to give. I enjoyed visiting my aunt Mary Lou and my grandmother. Their wisdom and life stories gave me spiritual dimension. I will forever be in their debt.

Example 9: Family Issues, Holiday Negotiating

Years ago my husband lost his job. Since we were financially strapped, we approached our families to let them know we would be holding back on birthday and Christmas presents. Instead of traditional presents, we brought food to share.

In the beginning, most of the family members were hesitant with the change. Some exchanged presents. But as time passed, everyone realized many holiday celebrations have morphed into a free-for-all celebration of spending.

In my view, special occasions should be about honoring and celebrating each other's connections more than buying gifts. I'm not dismissing gifts altogether. Every family has to find their own comfort zone. Besides, children look forward to birthday presents and other gift-giving holidays. Creatively give of yourself everyday. This is where you will truly make a difference in someone's life.

Example 10: Family Issues, Pettiness

I heard this story from a family member. Relatives from New York were visiting their family in Rhode Island. The mom told her oldest son they were entertaining their aunt and uncle at a near-by restaurant. He was invited, but since dad felt they could not arrive until 5:30 p. m. maybe he should not attend.

She said, "You know how your father is. He wants his supper early. Your younger brother would be able to make it since he and his wife would be available for 5:00 p. m.

Unknown to anyone, during the week, the oldest son was meeting his father at the local donut shop. After chatting for a few minutes, the son expressed to his dad he felt put out that he did not want to wait a half hour for him and his wife to arrive at the restaurant. He told his father he would have loved to join the New York relatives at the family gathering. His dad was astounded. He did not know anyone was being excluded. He made it clear he wanted his children together.

I have a rule of thumb; if someone is speaking for someone else I make sure I address the source. It is better to face the truth than to hang on to the words of someone else's interpretations of what the truth is.

FAVORITISM

Everyone knows someone who has a parent or relative who exhibits favoritism toward one child at the expense of the other siblings. Favoritism exists, and some people are either oblivious or they may not care how their favoritism harms others. They do not understand the effects it has on a child's development—the favorite or otherwise. Below are a few snippets to help one through favoritism's sharp edges.

• Do not take family exclusions as personal rejections (it is what it is). You have no power over it.

• Do not persist on seeking what is emotionally owed to you or place blame on others.

• Accept that people are going to do lousy things sometimes—for their own empty reasons.

• A rule of thumb: Ask for nothing more than a person is willing to give.

•Do not ruin your life by fuming about things someone is unwilling to give. Try to accept and anticipate an individual's limitations.

• Do your best and follow your steadfast principles.

Example 1: Favoritism, Siblings

In Albany, New York, the Prescotts raised three children, Sue, Albert, and Kyle. Kyle, the youngest child, happened to be the favorite of both parents. Sue and Albert did not allow their parent's favoritism of Kyle to taint their relationship with each other.

When their father passed away, he stated in his will that all his financial investments and material possession would go to his loving wife. But if she did not survive him, the estate would be divided equally between his three children.

A few years after their father's passing, Sue and Albert noticed their mother and Kyle seemed distant. Sue and Albert asked Kyle if he had a problem he would like to talk about. They both remarked how he had not invited them to his home lately and they rarely went out to lunch. Kyle brushed off their questions. He told his brother and sister he had been super busy.

Through the years, Sue and Albert only saw Kyle at holiday gatherings. As time went by, it became obvious their mother would subjectively compare them to Kyle. Regularly she would boast how Kyle was such a special person and he had unique qualities that they lacked.

Over the next two years their mother's health declined. Sue helped with household chores and took their mother to doctor appointments. Albert and Kyle did odd jobs and repairs around the house. The three siblings filled in each other's schedules as needed.

After their mother passed away, Kyle inherited his mother's entire estate. The thoughtful inheritance for her one child became an insult toward Sue and Albert. They felt distraught their mother thought so little of them.

Even though their mother was not always rational or fair, Kyle encouraged his mother to think as unkindly as she wanted. He never stated to his mother that his siblings were responsible adults and that they participated in caring for her as much as he. Kyle has passed up a chance to form deep connection to his siblings. Sue and Albert have to face what is.

Example 2: Favoritism, Personality Differences

My girlfriend has two children. Her son is energetic and adorable. Her daughter is quiet and observant. Whether at the grocery store, church function, or anywhere there is a crowd, someone will lavish him with attention. Her daughter tends to blend in the background. And it hurts her to see her daughter being left out.

As I mentioned before, people are thoughtless when it comes to siblings. They compliment or compare siblings without regard to how these comparisons might hurt the other party. I note this often when people ooh and ah over a baby and shamelessly treat the older siblings as if they were non-existent.

My friend did not want to diminish her son's accomplishments. She realizes her son deserves all the accolades he can get. She spoke to her daughter about her brother's popularity. She brought to her attention he is like the puppy or kitten everyone notices.

She explained their differences and that sometimes her goodness and kindness may not be seen by everyone. But she knows she is a wonderful person. They also had a conversation about how she feels when people fawn over her brother and neglect her. She keeps the dialogue perpetually open and shows her children how to appreciate each other.

To take her daughter out of her brother's charm circle, the mother enrolled her in activities that she would excel in. They joined a mother and daughter club. She knows that the families that bonds together stay together.

FAMILY AND BORROWING MONEY

Lending money or material possessions between family members definitely corrupts family peace. When a family member wants to borrow money, think of it as a gift. If, perchance, you received the money promised—jump for joy.

Suppose you cannot afford to lend (give) money– then you should not overextend yourself. From my experience, there is dissension within the family whenever a borrower breaches an IOU contract. Try your best not to go there.

Example 1: Borrowing Money, Obligation

A woman lent her daughter a considerable amount of money. Eight months passed without the daughter giving her a dime toward the loan. The mother felt her daughter was not going to fulfill her obligation. It bothered her, but she said nothing.

When her husband lost his job, she mentioned to her daughter they needed the money. She would like her to start paying back the loan at the reasonable rate of $50.00 a month. Her daughter felt she was being selfish and money hungry.

I call this a twister. No one is satisfied and feelings are trampled from both sides. Unless you are in the loan business, think twice about lending money.

Example 2: Borrowing Money, Moocher

My girlfriend's brother-in-law has always been financially irresponsible. He never seems to have enough money to fulfill his obligations. Lately, he has filed for bankruptcy. Currently, with his third wife, he is mooching off his seventy-five-year-old father. He does not pay rent or help with any of the household expenses. She heard he is depleting his father's bank account.

Somehow family members should intervene. Her father-in-law should be protected. What will happen to this elderly man when he no longer has any savings? The son is definitely a deadbeat (see Chapter XV, "Unfulfilled People").

BICKERING AFFECTS CHILDREN

Everyone should be cognitive of their tone of voice, especially in a child's presence. Children see and hear everything and bury their feelings. Everything they witness changes them and touches them dramatically—possibly on the cellular level. Even silly bickering could distress a child.

Be aware of your verbiage. Do not speak when you feel out of control. And note that angry silences in proximity to children are also equally profound. If, perchance, a child is within earshot of an argument, make sure he or she witnesses a successful reconciliation.

Think about it. Children are seldom interested in who is right or wrong in an argument. They simply want it to stop. If one person insists on bickering, remove yourself from the situation.

Example 1: Bickering, Parents Divorcing

Molly's parents recently separated—her dad initiated it. Molly is having difficulty coming to grips with the situation. She asked her dad to give her details of why he is divorcing her mother. He told her it involves personal information between him and her mother, and he will not speak to her about it.

At times, when Molly's mother is in an angry state, she will trash-talk Molly's father. Her words are destructive. Molly has told her mother she does not want to hear anything bad about her dad, but every once in a while, mom insists on venting her coarse accusations.

She told me she wants to walk away from her mother. She hesitates since her mom is already in a major crisis; she would feel guilty making her mother suffer further.

If someone asks someone not to do something disrespectful, and they choose to do it anyway, walking away is an appropriate response. Molly should express why she feels the way she feels. Clearly explain to mom, "I asked you not to trash-talk dad. You are hurting our relationship and I want you to stop. If you insist, I will be visiting you less often."

Molly does not necessarily need to know the details of her parent's breakup. Their relationship is a private matter between her parents. Children should not be burdened with painful situations that do not concern them. When it comes to parents, it is best for a child to concentrate on his or her life and maintain a neutral stance.

Example 2: Bickering, Parent and Children's Boundaries

A man whose wife divorced him three years ago spent three years relating to his daughter without incident.

Everything changed when he found out, through his daughter, that a good friend of his moved into his house. Suddenly the pieces to the puzzle fit together and he realized this man was in the picture long before his divorce. He feels doubly hurt and betrayed that his ex thought of him as a disposable object.

Unfortunately, when his daughter delivered the news, his behavior was less than stellar and he made comments that were inappropriate. Now his daughter does not want to see him; he misses her terribly.

Both parents should be dialing down their drama. He needs to call his ex and daughter and humbly apologize and ask both of them to forgive him. He should promise his daughter he will never speak ill of her mother again. A child should not be expected to take sides. All children should be free from their parent's problems.

Example 3: Bickering, Unacceptable Behavior

Let us pretend you have three sisters-in-law. One sister-in-law named Vickie is a troublemaker who lives out of state. She has a habit of talking about people behind their backs—most of what she has to say is untrue.

For the past two years you and your husband, Nicholas, have been taking care of your mother-in-law's finances. A week ago you heard through one of your sisters-in-law that Vickie is making strong accusations against you. She is telling everyone in the family you and your husband are stealing from Mom's savings. The end result is that your mother-in-law began questioning your honesty.

I am sure this is not the first time Vickie has lied. Who knows why Vickie has a personal agenda or if she is even mentally competent? The fact remains you cannot control her behavior.

As a choice, you could confront Vickie. Tell her you have no intention of listening to her attacks. And then switch to a lower gear and change the subject. Be prepared, she will probably blow her top. Maybe under the circumstances it is best to enlist a family member as an ally. Also, it is time to hire a lawyer. He or she could formally show the family, Vickie included, your legal documents and prove to others you are handling Mom's finances accurately.

Example 4: Bickering, Emotional Manipulation
Janie is the mother of three daughters. She withholds her affection from the child she feels has not co-operated with her ideas. She later makes contrived comments to her other two daughters against their sister and expects them to gang up on her to set their sister straight.

Janie justifies her actions. She feels she is teaching her children the consequences of making wrong choices—a choice she does not approve of. She has raised her daughters to reflect the same attitude. In time, the vicious circle will make a permanent scar on the entire family. Who knows? One day Janie's daughters may gang up on mom and withhold their affection from her.

CHILDREN AND MEASURING

Society tends to homogenize children—wanting them to fit into a particular mold. Sometimes parents do the same. They do not see their children's harmonic energy flow. They want their children to have all their positive attributes, exclude the negative ones, and behave exactly the way they imagine their children should behave.

If you feel this action is warranted, you are observing your children outside your life instead of being part of your life. Parents must understand children become the reflection of the attention they receive from their parents. No child is a parent's future clone or a vision of one's misguided dream.

Revere your child's uniqueness and frailties. Note how a child instinctively wants to make a connection to his or her guardian, to share joy, to love, and to be loved. Every child has something to give and so do you. Feel the power in your relationship. It is a bond that will stay with you forever.

PRESSURING CHILDREN

Personally, I do not think it is right to pressure children into physical contact or affection. Children are like lightning rods—they absorb unfiltered adult energy. Who knows the reason someone may make your child feel uncomfortable? Honor your children's boundaries. This practice will help your children to understand their sense of self and to feel safe to speak-out about inappropriate behaviors.

Questions:

Do you live your life through your children and become angry when they do not make the choices you feel they should have made? Do you know how to step back from a family drama without becoming the engine driving the boat?

• Answer the questions honestly, and remember you are not the only sensitive person.

CHAPTER X

A bountiful spirit endures life's inconveniences
with an all-knowing smile.

THE COMPLEXITY OF MEN AND WOMEN

Both men and women take their stand in society seriously. Women experience their relationships internally. They find solace by relating their problems to others—their communication skills are excellent. They are face-to-face type of people and hands-on. Women question why and how situations exist. Sometimes they may even rehash a situation until it loses its initial value. When women do not feel appreciated, they become depressed or may withdraw physically and emotionally.

Men experience their relationships externally. They communicate in short increments. For example, they enjoy sitting with men watching sports—a shoulder-to-shoulder thing. They look at the facts connected to a problem with an uncomplicated eye. Their masculine energy treats a problem as a command. They rarely give in to roadblocks.

He will do what he has to do and meet a situation with a vengeance and possibly appear curt and insensitive. Many times, under stress they will fight or take flight. In a heated moment, he rarely shows his softer side. His attitude is full steam ahead, and then without a thought, he immediately closes the door to his aggravation.

Society perceives men and women as separate entities. To this day women are not paid an equal salary. Some people believe men are to lead while women should be subservient and take a passive role. Naturally, men and woman are different, nevertheless, that does not mean either should be constrained or penalized to play a certain role or be judged by others.

Example: Women

Abby told me she had a huge fight with her husband. It started over the long weekend. Her husband had his buddies at their house non-stop. She felt like she was the hired cook, waitress, and housekeeper. She did not say anything because she did not want to cause a scene, but she steamed inside. Needless to say, her husband never noticed her moody demeanor.

Later in the middle of the week, after she washed the kitchen floor, her husband walked on it with his muddy boots. She told me she lost her mind and continually nagged and fumed about his inconsideration.

I asked, "Why would a muddy floor bother you to such an extreme?"

Her eyes opened wide. It was as though a light bulb flashed. She said, "Now, I realize it was not the muddy floor that bothered me. It was being treated like the hired help over the past weekend."

She placed her feelings on the back burner and allowed her issues to grind at her. She could have asked for help or mentioned she felt used. Her husband is not a mindreader. He was having fun. How was he supposed to know she was not?

Example: Men

Men rarely ask for assistance and many detest asking for directions. To fight off their tensions, they may throw Rumplestiltskin hissy fits in the hope that a problem will disappear. Whenever my husband does this, he reminds me of the farmer's scarecrow trying to ward of the birds from the garden. For the fifty years I have known him, he never tires of practicing this tactic.

MEN AND WOMEN IN CONFLICT

The book *Men are from Mars and Women are from Venus* explains the mental and emotional diversities between men and women. It shows how both men and women get caught in their own masquerade—a position where they become obliquely unconscious of the other person's representation.

It is easy for her to tell herself his yearnings are simple while hers are complex. It is easy for him to tell himself she will get over it as he closes the door to all discussions.

Both men and women inflict emotional pain on those they love, since they know where their loved one's "Achilles' heal" is located. Each partner needs to reflect, comprehend, and validate his or her action and words. As I mentioned before, true dialogue begins without conflict.

Sincerely express yourself from the heart and feel each other's devotion. Clarify what is bothering you, in a loving way, instead of arguing. Dismissing a problem will only make another playground for ridicule. By showing a true interest in a relationship, one has already triggered a peaceful solution—introducing a flow to your dialogue.

Reward yourself and your partner with comfort. Castaway predigest views. Respect individuality and your connection to the present moment. Practice honesty, awareness, and compassion. By doing so you will touch something in yourself—something you could not have experienced through the ego.

When one engages in inappropriate behavior or deliberately isolates him- or herself, the relationship becomes blocked. At this point, you will find yourself latching onto negative traits or buzzwords—closing the opening for the new.

The trick to all dialogue is never to assume anything or interrupt or interpret each other. Be mindful of your defenses; draw out the truth of a matter. Do not measure the right or wrong of an outcome. Train yourself to be selfishly selfless. Listen and watch how you react to a given situation. If for some reason you are afraid to express yourself, look further into your motives. Note that each situation—within the moment—has its own perfection. The perfection is not a solution (solutions are relative). Perfection is sharing dialogue.

Do not get into a passive-aggressive habit. This tactic shows anger. When you hear a person say he or she will talk about something later, that means "later." Do follow through on a time scheduled—dismissing a discussion would be an avoidance.

I like to point out that there is fine line to being oneself and being rigid. Rigidity has its own kind of ultimatum—such as "deal with it or else." Question if you have this type of mentality. It is a way to face "what is" head on.

Questions:

How much does your relationship mean to you? Do both of you care whether your relationship thrives or not? Is your relationship worth saving and why?

• Note if someone is disrespecting you, this is your cue to respect yourself.

SELF-DEFENSIVE AND ABUSIVE RELATIONSHIPS

In truth, some people's defenses rise easily and others squabble for the sake of squabbling. Know it is impossible to resolve a sarcastic individual's offensiveness—their peculiarities belong to them. Never tolerate emotional bullying or any behavior that whitewashes one's essence. And never allow insincere apologetic platitudes to undue an abuser's short fuse. Do not try to fix a volatile situation. The average person is not professionally or emotionally equipped to conjure the reasons why some people lash out.

Years ago I heard a conversation that went something like this. A woman mentioned she felt bad for people who did not know how to treat others. If someone was mean-spirited to her, she would dismiss their attitude because she felt they did not know any better. Her friend told her people have to be trained. When a person is being disrespectful, one needs to confront that person. How else will he or she learn the consequences of their actions?

The difference between being judgmental and live-and-let-live is the depth of one's humility. When someone is aggressive and asks you a question that makes you feel uncomfortable, deflect the question by turning it around. Make an innocuous query and be focused and direct. This gives a person a chance to rethink their phraseology and a chance for you to move on to another topic.

Above all, do not allow someone's negativity to rub off on you. Life is too short to get caught in someone else's tangled thinking. If someone is trying to manipulate you emotionally, note the noise you feel. Notice how your body internally shutters.

To break the habit of verbal or physical abuse, whether you are the abuser or a victim—one should consider psychiatry, hypnotherapy, or other alternative forms of motivation to put an end to this invasive habit.

Example 1: Abusive Relationship, Controlling a Loved One

Jeff has a high-powered job on Wall Street. He is a deacon at his church and a member of the school committee. To many of his neighbors and colleagues, he appears to be a perfect husband. In the public arena, he showers his wife, Minnie, with attention and compliments. It is not a surprise most people immediately like him.

At home, he is a completely different man. He is verbally sharp and mean. He monitors his wife's telephone calls, hacks into her daily emails, and interrogates her about her day. He even checks the caller ID unit to track incoming calls.

She is not allowed to go outside and speak to the neighbors unless he is nearby. If she happens to be engaged in a conversation too long, he harasses her every five seconds until she finally gives into his whim. Minnie and Jeff do not have a relationship. They are in a master slave situation. Both of them need of counseling.

Example 2: Abusive Relationship,
Degrading a Loved one

Archie asked his colleague, Georgia, to give him the recipe for her sour cream cake. She made the cake for their last business meeting and everyone raved about it. He mentioned he and his wife were planning a special dinner party the following Saturday and he thought the sour cream cake would make a great addition to the party. He added her cake was the best cake he had ever tasted.

Weeks later Georgia asked Archie about the dinner party? Archie abruptly raised his voice. He told Georgia his stupid good-for-nothing wife forgot to put a special ingredient in the cake and she ruined the evening.

Georgia noticed this was not the first time Archie had degraded his wife. Somehow, his wife never seems to measure up. She rarely does anything right. She either wears ill-fitting clothes, she was not graceful, or she was making his life difficult.

Georgia is cordial with Archie at work, but she keeps her distance from his negative and explosive personality.

Example 3: Abusive Relationship,
Mistreating a Loved One

During the holiday months, Bert told me he was weary of being his girlfriend's battering ram. He explained she liked to make a joke of him in front of their friends. When he complained and asked her to stop, she told him he is overly sensitive and she cannot understand why he does not want to be a sidekick to her charming wit. Besides, no one takes her comments seriously—it is all in good fun. She does not seem to care that he is fed up with her insensitive remarks.

If anyone is the object of humiliation or continual public put downs, perhaps there is a one sided relationship here. This woman needs a reality check with actual consequences. Obviously, she does not know where to draw a boundary line. If she does not stop treating her guy like a ninny, he will have to make a decision to stay with the status quo or to move on. His choice.

Example 4: Abusive Relationship

Beatrice, a teenager, was asked to join a girls' club. She had to go through a ritual to join. She accepted. The ritual was disgusting and now she is ashamed of herself. She does not want to be part of the group anymore and she told her parents about the episode.

I think this young lady was brave to open her heart to her parents. And as far as I am concerned, the ringleader should be reported to the school or police. When people rally together, a clique can be broken and make a negative situation or nasty individual's powerless.

Example 5: Abusive Relationship, Psychopathic Personality

I had a friend with a Dr. Jekyll and Mr. Hyde type of personality. When she was in a good mood, she was exciting and fun. When she was in a bad mood she was mean-spirited and felt anything goes. It took me years before I realized her tolerance for "anything goes" was escalating. I finally became burnt out.

One day I got the courage to interject without being confrontational. I told her she was being hurtful, and I gave her examples. She replied, "Accept me as I am."

Although I was reluctant, we parted ways. I still miss her. I do not miss her antics.

Example 6: Abusive Relationship, Confronting a Friend's Behavior

I heard this story from a friend's friend—let us say his name is Barney. Barney's neighbor/friend has anger problems. In the past, on several occasions, he saw him slap his son. One day his son ran away from home to his house and told him he did not want to go home. Later, when the child's dad came to the house to retrieve his son he acted gracious and friendly. However, when Barney looked out his picture window, he saw his friend pulling his son's hair and then throwing him into the back seat.

When he confronted his friend about abusing his child, the man told him to mind his own business. Barney does not know what to do. He thought of calling the authorities, but he does not want to ruin their friendship.

There is a responsibility here. He must help Barney and his son. Be a true friend. Ask him to receive help and follow-up on this matter. Maybe he could volunteer to go with him. A counselor would be able to offer assistance that this man cannot receive through a friendship. Do not allow this type of behavior to stay hidden. If the man does not cooperate, he should be reported.

Example 7: Verbally Abusive

Clarence had a foul mouth. He could not speak unless he was using vulgar language. He would say the "f" word constantly and when someone asked him to cool down, his toxic behavior would escalate.

Some people cannot say a sentence without cussing. They do not understand or care how uncomfortable they make others feel. Confronting this type of person probably would not be effective, and it could be dangerous—there seems to be underlining issues of anger here.

The people around him should bolster themselves emotionally. Maybe even get support through a counselor. No one deserves to live under a cloud of feeling rotten in order for someone else to feel temporarily better.

Exercise:
Stare at a self-defensive person calmly. Ask that individual to repeat his or her remark. Keep your mind silent. By studying this person's reality, you will find the correct manner and right answer to make a profound remark. Or at least, for yourself, you could defuse a volatile situation or end a negative cycle. It is not so much you are trying to change someone; you are acknowledging you deserve better.

Questions:
Does your partner try to brainwash you? Has anyone ever tried to physically or verbally attack you? Do you apologize continually and unnecessarily? Are you a person who is easily agitated? Have you ever struck another person in anger to control a situation?

• Think about the answers to these questions. Look to restore your confidence, and realize you have power to guide your life. Do not block your spirit's intimacy.

Relationship Ethics

No one can walk in another person shoes, but one can surmise how another person may feel. My friend's husband was unfaithful seven years ago. When she found out, he ended the affair. She told me there is not a day that goes by without her wondering if he will have another affair. And she cannot find it in her heart to trust him.

Cheaters do not seem to realize the true scope of what they have done. Once they stop their affair, they move on with their lives. As for the person suffering, it does not always happen that way. There are no get-out-of-jail-free cards to make a relationship immediately come back from a cruel deception. This couple has a rocky road ahead of them. Everything has changed.

Trust is gone and trust has to rebuild slowly. First they will have to open their energy fields to each other and become as one. Second they will have to allow the past to disintegrate before they can walk together on the same road—honesty matters. Possibly, a qualified counselor may need to intervene.

Example: Relationship Ethics, Remorse

Travis had a serious girlfriend in his home town. When he went to college, he fell in love with a classmate. After months of lying to both his girlfriend and his new flame, he went through a period of self-reflection. He told his girlfriend the truth. With remorse, he explained he did not know why he made the decision he made and he was deeply sorry for treating her so badly.

They resumed their relationship. When he made arrangements to travel overseas with friends, his girlfriend told him she did not trust him and she could not be with him right now. He does not understand why she needs her space. He has apologized and he feels he is a different person now. He does not know what else he can do to show her how remorseful he feels.

With relationships, there are two sides to please. In many incidents, past behaviors become the predictor of future results. Also, relationships are not like press conferences where you can make a statement, say "sorry," and walk away. One has to offer support, wait for the other to weigh in, and actively listen.

I think being apart will give both of parties the opportunity to reflect upon their trust issue. In the wake of betrayal—it is not just about time—one has to tirelessly demonstrate how much he or she really cares.

Example: Relationship Ethics, Repeating Negative Behavior

Nine years ago, a woman forgave her husband for his indiscretion with a married co-worker. The affair ended when the woman's husband confronted the man and told him to stop seeing his wife. Since the deed was out in the open, her husband informed her of the situation. He apologized and promised he would never break her heart again. She forgave her husband—it took two years to fully trust him.

Recently, she discovered he has been secretly meeting a different co-worker after work and on weekends. He claims this new woman does not mean anything to him. He swears he his not having an affair. He only kept the other woman a secret because she has a jealous nature from the previous experience.

It seems to me the woman's husband behaves the way he wants to behave until his wife catches him. He has no regard for her feelings or the harm he is causing. He has the nerve to justify his current problem by branding his wife as the perpetrator.

He needs a reality check and to stop making excuses. He expects her to get over it and not allow her feelings of betrayal to interfere with their marriage? It is time this man owns up to his behavior. Counseling for both parties is much needed.

Validating True Relationships

True relationships have an intimacy that extends to the total person. Even though sharing each other's life journey may not always be an easy fit, one has a choice to make it engaging. Relationships are never built on expectations; one mutually respects one another's boundaries and sensitivities.

Some people force detrimental relationships on themselves—talking themselves into something in spite of the little voice whispering "this is not right" or "too soon," which incidentally, is the first hint to be more decisive. Practice awareness or you will unconsciously seek individuals who will gladly take advantage of you.

One partner cannot make all the compromises. If so, the relationship becomes empty. Confrontations are quibbles over an illusion—a matter that has no substance. Become aware of the "us" in your relationships. And recognize all relationships are the mirrors of one's inner self—another dimension of who we are.

Break unhealthy relationship patterns. Realize that all destructive relationships are not about choosing bad people; they are about making foolish decisions for improper reasons. Take care of yourself and honor the sacredness of your life's journey.

Example 1: Relationship, Inappropriateness

Joseph, Nancy's husband's childhood friend of twenty years, who lives out of state, has been visiting them for the past three years. He stays with them four days once a year. He is crude and rude. He frequently uses foul language and degrades women while she is in the room. The other day Nancy's husband said something inappropriate to her. She was greatly offended and she abruptly left the room.

That evening she confronted her husband. She told him she was upset with his remark. He apologized—admitting he was wrong. She mentioned she does not like the influence Joseph has on him and for future visits, she would rather Joseph check into a nearby hotel.

Sometimes the simplest solution to a precarious situation is to take the problem out of the equation. Changing the present condition will help Nancy's husband to understand the depth of her comfort zone and the reality of Joseph's remarks.

Example 2: Relationship, Friendships Change

Let us suppose a dear childhood friend—whose family moved to another state—asked you to store her belongings in your parent's basement while you both attended college. At college you shared several classes together and lived in the same dorm.

However, after both of you had settled in, your friend blatantly ignored you. In the few attempts to contact her, she replied, "I'm busy" or "I'll call you back." Worst of all, you were excluded from get-togethers with mutual friends. At the end of the semester you want to return her things. Needless to say, you are not in the mood to do your childhood friend any more favors.

Childhood friendships do falter; one has to change with the flow. Be cordial, but make it clear, possibly with a date, you would like her personal possessions retrieved from your parent's basement. Do not allow her to argue the point. Obviously, you do not have a close relationship with her anymore. Now is the moment to follow your truth. Since your friend is acting like a stranger, you too can move forward just like she did.

Example: Relationship, Trying to Change Someone

Rose had been friends with Gloria for thirty years. As children, they went on family vacations, lived in the same college dorm, and later, rented their first apartment together. When Rose received a large inheritance from her grandmother, she retired and moved to New York City. She kept herself busy by volunteering her time to various charities. Rose and Gloria continually stayed in touch through emails and telephone calls.

Rose asked Gloria to visit her in New York City for a week. She had a wonderful itinerary scheduled. The evening they planned to go to one of the charity events Rose complained to Gloria about her outfit. She did not care for her taste in clothes. Nor did she feel the color she was wearing was right for her. She furthered her grievance by commenting her style of dress made her look dowdy. Gloria shook off Rose's comments. She did not want to ruin their plans.

At the charity ball, Gloria enjoyed the festivities and meeting new people. The following day Rose told Gloria she wanted her to buy her new clothes for the rest of the week's itinerary. She made it clear she felt uncomfortable being with Gloria with the clothes she had brought from their hometown.

Rose could have been more careful of Gloria's feelings by suggesting they go shopping together. And mention how she would love to buy her clothes to wear on her vacation. They would have had fun and the gesture would have showed Gloria how much Rose honored their friendship.

Rose giving a subjective opinion about Gloria's clothes did not serve anyone's purpose. Rose has lost something in her heart that is very dear—the connection to Gloria's energy. They no longer have a close friendship.

Questions:
Are you in a damaging relationship? Are your delusions the glue that keeps your relationship alive?

• When you are not clear, you cannot commit to your spirit.

ENABLERS

Enablers are people who give authority and power to another person. These super-sensitive, insecure, and emotionally immature individuals wait for someone to take advantage of them. They are seduced by people who magnify their self doubts while making them feel they are needed. Note when you do not follow your spirit you smolder underneath. Living this way stifles one's experiences.

No one should allow a loved one to exploit them. Take a long hard look at your relationships. Recognize the difference between those who are kind or self-centered, and then relate to those people accordingly.

NEEDINESS AND "POOR ME" SYNDROME

Needy people try to push their mess onto others. And a "poor me" person does the same. If an individual is zapping your space, it is time you confronted him or her. You will be helping yourself and the needy person as well.

I think the following analogy says it all. Two friends had not seen each other for year. They met at a neighborhood coffee shop. The first friend went on and on about herself for a half hour. Finally, she realized she had been doing all the talking.

She gestured to her friend. "I'm sorry I've been talking about myself for a half hour. Now it is your turn to talk about me."

Example: Needy Person

Brian is incapable of communicating with another person. He feels unhappy and goes on and on about how his life is full of problems. No one seems to understand his plight. He rarely asks anyone about his or her day. After all, his day is such a mess.

Create a new practice with a needy person. Train him or her the way you would train a toddler—be firm, friendly, and unashamed. Tell this person how you feel and quickly move on to another subject. Who knows? He or she may listen.

Example: Cling-on

Let us suppose there is a woman at work who will not leave you alone. She emails you throughout the day with trivial details. She forwards you jokes and messages from her friends that you have no interest in reading. When you do not respond, she stops by your cubicle to check on you.

While you are working, she stands over you and interrupts your work flow. She pressures you about having lunch together or asks you personal questions that invade your privacy. You have tried to defuse the situation by conjuring excuses. Often, you have subtly told her she is invading your space. She ignores everything you say. Nothing seems to give her a hint.

Cling-ons do not honor hints. You have to state your position simply and clearly. Tell her you expect her to respect your personal boundaries. Let her know how uncomfortable she is making you feel. Explain you do not like emails or forwarded messages. Mention that her interruptions are breaking your concentration and diminishing your job performance.

Watch her demeanor. Stop and wait in between your comments to check if she is absorbing your dialogue. Stay in the moment. Then move forward when you know she has absorbed one sentence—repeat as needed. If you are unable to change your colleague's attitude, maybe you will have to take the next step and speak to your supervisor.

Questions:

Do you cross another person's boundaries? Do you feel someone else should make you happy? Have you ever followed through with an action that you knew in your heart was not in the best interest for you or someone else?

• The choices made from the ego's point of view are bound to make your life complicated and difficult.

CHAPTER XI

Silence dissipates the power of unpleasantness.

FORGIVENESS IS AN ACTION

Forgiveness is the cancellation of a condition in your mind that prevents the flow of love. It means eradicating resentments or penalizing someone for a wrong you feel he or she has made against you. One cannot move forward by focusing on resentment. In retrospect, I do not know of anyone who has not unintentionally made a hurtful remark or done something that will cause another person to suffer—it is inescapable. Let us examine different degrees of forgiveness.

First let us consider the mini-forgiveness. For instance, if your friend was supposed to meet you at 10:00 a.m. and arrived at 12:00 p. m.—you would consider that mini-forgiveness. But if your friend promised to take you to a party and never showed up, you would consider that thoughtless—a medium forgiveness. One is not as likely to brush that type of incident aside so easily—although obviously, both issues should be addressed. Again, if your partner betrayed your trust, and you were to forgive him or her that would be a giant forgiveness.

Ah... let me take two steps backward. Can forgiveness be measured? Forgiveness does not mean allowing individuals to casually dismiss his or her mistake. It is more like connecting the dots in a child's coloring book. The picture is complete when both parties own a problem, work on a solution, and let go of the illusions connected to the past.

Though you may not agree with the behavior of another person, your decision to forgive releases you from holding onto destructive feelings—resentment. Live in the present moment to conquer future regrets. Do not become a long-term victim or a martyr. Free yourself from the expectation you thought a person was going to fulfill.

Remember true forgiveness is not taking on a superior attitude while the other person is supposed to carry the guilt. If so, it would be more like throwing a Nerf ball. It is soft and squishy, but does not travel very far. Self-forgiveness has the same concept. Take responsibility. Be patient. Wipe the slate clean and respect yourself.

Example 1: Forgiveness is an Action

Throughout Jennifer's childhood, her father traveled a great deal. And while he was home, he ignored her unless he was cussing. Around the age of eleven, she emotionally distanced herself from her father. Through the years she avoided her dad as much as possible.

At the age of twenty, Jennifer's mother planned to give her husband a fiftieth birthday party. Jennifer felt this would be a good time to make a conscious effort to rekindle her relationship with her father. She met him at his favorite restaurant—a neutral place.

Jennifer expressed how she felt as a child. She vented she did not feel her dad loved her. He was standoffish and she did not understand why he cussed all the time. She craved his attention, but his volatile personality made her upset. She took a deep breath and paused for a moment. Her tone changed. She told him she was tired of living in the past and holding a grudge.

He downcast his eyes and hung his head. He cleared his throat and his voice quivered. He told her he was deeply sorry for their wasted days. He admitted he was wrong. In his youth, he was immature and life's every day pressures made him feel overwhelmed. He did not know how to cope.

He made it clear he was not making excuses for his faults. He hoped she would realize he had changed. He asked Jennifer to forgive him. He smiled and touched her hand. He told her he would like to start a new relationship with her.

Jennifer could have rehashed the past, giving her father lengthy details of her past wounds. She could have acted like a martyr, shown a superior attitude, or complained profusely about his parenting skills.

An egoistic attitude would have broken their energy flow and taken the life out of the present moment. She knew seeing her father crawl for one revengeful moment would not transform their relationship. True forgiveness begins as a change is taking place. If each person honestly commits to change, the silent place in one's heart has a way of caressing both parties.

Example 2: Forgive Yourself
Rosemary and Leo are the parents of two children. Their son, Jason, was a bookworm. He excelled in academic achievements. Their daughter, Julia, enjoyed the arts and

social interaction. As much as Jason excelled in school, Julia barely managed to pass from one grade to the other.

Rosemary and Leo nagged Julie constantly. They tried every parental trick imaginable to coerce Julia into being a better student. She simply refused to apply herself. She felt since she planned on being an artist her grades did not mean that much to her.

After years of urging Julia to be more like Jason, Julia's parents sent her to a private boarding school. The day Rosemary and Leo took Julia to boarding school she felt isolated and abandoned. She wept as she said goodbye.

Her parents felt terrible. They were going to miss her bubbly personality. Through the next few months, their relationship became painfully distant. On school vacations and holiday breaks, Julia refused to go home.

Toward the end of the school season, Rosemary and Leo realized their concern for their daughter was misplaced. They accepted that each child was experiencing life through distinct avenues of thought. Rosemary and Leo hated themselves for making a decision that took their daughter from them. They asked Julia to forgive them. She did.

However, they could not forgive themselves. Yes, they will never be able to recapture the year they lost. But by Rosemary and Leo dwelling on the past, they failed to live in the present. They will have to forgive themselves before they can begin a new relationship with their daughter.

When they forgive themselves, their egos will stop measuring past events. Through dialogue, they will open their energy fields and this newness will secure their relationship.

Example 3: Forgiveness, A Broken Promise

Edna enjoys filling in her days by volunteering her services. She will help anyone from a family member to a stranger at a moments notice. Needless to say, she overextends herself so much that she neglects to keep her promises. When she finds herself in a bind, she picks and chooses the promises that suit her momentary mood—even though someone may have counted on her availability. In a snap, she has been known to cancel obligations at the last minute or dismiss fulfilling a commitment without notification.

After being disappointed with Edna's lack of commitment, Ginny, Edna's cousin, brings Edna's behavior to her attention. Confronted, Edna becomes defensive. She shruggs her shoulders and glares at her cousin. With a spark in her voice, she make sit clear to Ginny that she has no right to complain.

Edna feels she should be left off the hook when she occasionally misrepresents herself. Ginny learned Edna has limitations. If she needs to count on someone, it will not be Edna. Ginny knows she cannot change Edna. She can only change Ginny.

Example 4: Forgiving an Insensitive Remark

Before Tom left for David's barbecue party, David called and asked him to purchase a bag of charcoal briquettes. He told him the brand he wanted and he would pay him for his troubles when he arrived at the party. Tom stopped at three stores, and there were no charcoal briquettes in sight. The fourth store had the briquettes, but they did not have David's brand. Tom bought them—he felt he had wasted enough time looking for briquettes. When Tom handed the briquette bag to David, he reacted with a snide remark. "Tom don't you know how to follow directions?"

Tom was miffed. In the past, He had talked to David about his flippant insensitive remarks and David promised he would try to understand Tom's point of view. Tom abruptly pulled David aside. He told him he was sorry he tried to help him. He added he went to four stores before he found the briquettes. With a firm voice Tom expressed he wanted an immediate apology.

David put his arm on Tom's shoulder. He apologized. He also expressed he appreciated his tenacity to get the job done. No doubt, David and Tom are bound to have other misunderstandings, but their awareness to stay in the moment will keep their friendship growing and intact.

Example 5: Forgiveness and Distraughtness

Let us pretend while you were in another country for three months your wife had a brief affair. You felt distraught about the infidelity. You thought about getting a divorce, but after a few months of counseling, you reconciled.

From the bottom of your heart you forgave your wife. Then months into your new relationship she discovers she is pregnant with the other man's child. Now everything has changed. You know the father of the child will want to be part of his child's life—forever. And you will always be reminded of your wife's indiscretion.

Forgetting or pretending the fling never happened will not work. Your forgiveness has to come from a genuine peaceful place—where your relationship is deeper than before. You can never rewind the past by testing or blaming. You must—honestly love—love another man's child. Is it is possible for you to accept what is? Search within to find the answer. Do you forgive your wife or say good-by?

Example 6: Forgiveness and Truly Moving On

Divorced individuals may find it difficult to forgive a husband or wife who has wronged him or her. They literally take the behavior of their former partner personally instead of considering he or she made a choice. Blame, going on a guilt trip, thinking one could have done this or that to save a relationship is wishful thinking. Take a positive approach. Arm your heart with the present moment. This is where you will feel the safety of the warm circle of life—where infinite changes unfold.

Example 7: Forgiveness, People Do Stupid Things

This happened to a friend's daughter. Penny once had a close relationship with her cousin Elizabeth. When they were teenagers, they liked the same boy. The young man asked Penny out—making Elizabeth jealous. In a woebegone state, she spread nasty rumors about her. Consequently their relationship ended. Elizabeth has never apologized.

Now fast forward to the present moment. Penny received a Facebook "friend's request" from Elizabeth. Penny feels her cousin has nerve to attempt to repair their relationship in this fashion. Especially, since her cousin has not bothered to contact her in years.

Sometimes we do things as children without thinking. Possibly, Elizabeth could be unaware that her childish rant affected Penny so deeply. Elizabeth may not even notice if Penny returns her gesture. It is Penny's call. Does she take this opportunity to re-establish a new relationship with her cousin or allow a youthful experience to keep its grip on her forever?

Exercise:
Forgiveness comes from a silent place with intimacy. One cannot drag his or her past mishaps into the present moment. Find a sense of balance by speaking to a friend or counselor, meditate, recite a mantra, pray, or take long walks. These simple actions may help you find the road toward forgiveness.

Questions:
What does forgiveness mean to you? Are you ready to embark on a new beginning—leave the past in the past?
• Do not allow hate to fill your heart.

Psychopathic and Combative People

Psychopathic people live under a dark shadow. Through ignorance or arrogance, they live a one-dimensional life. They do not have the capacity to feel—anything. Their wrath keeps them locked in resentment and blame.

Some people feel one should forgive a predator, but not the deed. How does one forgive a predator's violation? Is it even possible? Everyone has to search within to find his or her answer.

I do know, eventually, individuals have to relieve themselves from the pain of a terrible moment in order to move forward. And since there are different levels of atrocities it may take continued professional help to free one from suffering. The worst thing one can do is seek revenge. It is an empty vessel. There is nothing to gain from it, and if anything, holding onto hateful moments tend to make matters worse.

I have forgiven perpetrators when they actively practice a new way of life and are genuinely sorry for their deeds.

Their new way of life also places them in a state of forgiveness—they become one with the universal energy flow.

VINDICTIVENESS

All of us know someone who has expressed his or her personal unhappiness about another individual. If people cannot confront a person who they feel is making them unhappy directly, they should not be talking about that person. Defaming another person is vicious and spiteful. Do not allow yourself to reinforce this negativity. If a person is talking behind someone's back, he or she is more than likely doing the same to you. When someone repeats what someone said about you, explain you do not want to hear it.

If you feel hate, anger, or resentment toward someone, it is an indication you need an attitude change. Stop depleting your energy. Instead of stewing, get to the bottom of the problem and put an end to the misunderstanding.

Example 1: Vindictiveness

Peter confessed to his sister, Eleanor, that he was the person who stole money from the neighbors' houses. His mother took the fall. She was arrested and served six months in jail. The family was torn apart, and each sibling was sent to a different foster home. She went to her grave with everyone thinking she did the deed.

Peter's confession brought back lousy memories of Eleanor's childhood—she is bitter and angry. Eleanor wants Peter to confess his act to the family. And if he does not come clean, she plans to tell all.

Eleanor needs to search within. What good would it do anyone to drag up a messy past that cannot be rectified? Nothing can change Eleanor's childhood, but she can sprinkle her brother with forgiveness. And give her brother a big hug. It will take both of them out of their darkness and bring them to healthier place.

Questions:
Have you ever had someone quote what another person said about you, and then they made you promise not to confront that person? Have you had individuals ask you to be a go-between to defuse a problem?

• Anytime someone is speaking for someone else, question his or her motive. Do not become part of another person's agenda.

DISLIKING SOMEONE

Do you know someone who has good intentions, but still grates on your nerves? Disliking someone should not make you feel horrible. Immediate likes and dislikes are natural. It is not an affliction to be cured. Be gracious to everyone in your path, and when you feel uncomfortable or irritated with someone, take a deep breath and walk away.

I would like to emphasize there is a difference between disliking someone and being prejudice. But first let me define prejudice: A preconceived and unreasonable judgment, or opinion, usually, an unfavorable one marked by suspicion, fear and intolerance.

Prejudicial acts are fear-based. It is as though one is in a coma-inducing state where his or her energy stagnates. This type of individual reflects his or her own insecurities and emptiness. There is no self-empowerment. Only through observing our own actions can one break the heavy shackles of prejudice. Free yourself from this learned space. Stop following the Hungry Ghost—see Chapter XV, "Unfulfilled People."

Example: Disliking Someone, Prejudice

This story is from the 1980s. My family always brought their vehicles to a neighborhood garage. On the wall, the mechanic had his new wife's grandchild's picture displayed at various ages—from infancy to four years old. The child happened to be black. The mechanic spoke about this grandchild with delight.

The mechanic's mother came to the garage every morning to do the daily receipts in the ledger. One day she pointed to the child's picture and made derogatory comments to me about the race of the child. No one was in the waiting room. I told her I did not agree with her; the conversation ended.

Later, when the mechanic approached me to tell me my car was ready, she looked at her son. She boasted how she had lunch with a mutual friend. She spouted with a superior air, "You know how he is... he mentions the black and white thing all the time, and I had to tell him to stop."

The mechanic looked at me. I could tell he was embarrassed for her. Both of us knew his mother was talking about this subject deliberately. But his mother did not know that we knew. Probably, she did not care. The only person she was fooling was herself. Soon the built-up hate in her heart will stop her son from wanting her in his life. The odd part is that she will likely never understand why.

Chapter XII

Delays are paused alliances sprinkled with research and compromise.

Chronological Time

Chronological time is a measurement calculated by minutes, hours, days, and years. In the pragmatic world, everyone sets the clock to go from one point to another. Most people feel life moves from the past, to the present, and to the future by time. However, we cannot measure love, joy, or dreams by time. If we try to, we will be sliding down the unhappy slippery slope of a psychological moment.

Psychological Moments

Before you start to understand the root of a psychological moment, let me define psychology: Psychology is a science that treats the mind and its aspects in an orderly fashion through investigation of the phenomena of an individual's conscious behavior. The origin behind a psychological moment—an illusion—transforms a concept of thinking and that thinking seems absolute.

I recognize a psychologically obsessive person by his or her actions. They seem spaced out—present but not present. I like the German philosopher, Gurdjieff. He wrote people live their life as if they were walking in a perpetual dream. They have an existence, but they are unaware of their actions and the uniqueness of their spirit.

Psychological moments are one of the hardest behaviors to eliminate. They are so imprinted in one's psyche they feel like a friend—familiar and comforting. For instance, do you remember how it feels when the doctor hits your knee with a rubber hammer? Your knee jumps spontaneously. Psychological moments are similar to a hammer hitting the knee—a reaction.

Note that psychological moments cannot stand by themselves. Think of the worst day of your life. Remember how the day felt directionless; how it dragged on. It seemed know matter where you turned or who you turned to no one could help you harness positive energy. An unbridled nervousness devoured the clearness in your heart making you feel exhausted physically and mentally.

Who do you think was in control of that psychological moment? It was you. You are the person who forced yourself to perpetuate a moment from the past and made it last for days, months or years. Recognize how your illusions support misplaced attachments of what if, hate, and anger.

To protect itself, the ego dodges the present moment with an all consuming power—resembling a hungry lioness before she catches her meal, focused and rigid. Search within. Do not wrap yourself around an illusion as if you were an infant in a swaddling blanket. Stay in a moment with a fresh attitude. Learn something about yourself. Question what is obstructing your progress. Take small steps—there is a vast datum waiting for your input. In a minute, everything could make sense. Do not give up. Find your voice.

There is an unfolding when awareness breaks an illusion. One may feel as though he or she is a frightened bird, and literally cannot function. To carry yourself through this period, make sure you take plenty of quiet time and space to adjust to the new you. Also, during your transition it is best not to overextend yourself socially.

Example 1: A Career Promotion with True Feelings

Let us suppose you receive a surprise promotion at work. A true feeling is a forward movement. The energy is clear. You bask in your accomplishment. You have a positive attitude and enjoy sharing your news with your family and friends.

A Career Promotion with Psychological Feelings

With a psychological feeling, you want to brag and gloat about your promotion. You feel you have an upper hand, and now you can measure your worth against your fellow employees.

Example 2: Psychological Thought Pattern

Suzann met her boyfriend at a concert. They immediately hit it off and throughout high school they were inseparable. She fell hopelessly in love. She spoke of her guy every waking moment. Just about everything revolved around him. Their friends called them the school's mascots.

Their relationship changed the summer her boyfriend visited his cousin in Maine. The first week they spoke to each other daily. A week later he took a short trip with his family to Europe. Slowly, their relationship began to unravel. At the end of the summer, his family moved to Maine and Suzann never saw him again.

Suzann refuses to forget her high school sweetheart. She believes no other man could measure-up to her lost love. To this day, she is stuck in a psychological trap. Although she is educated and has a great job, she has not grown emotionally or spiritually.

Example 3: Psychological, Beliefs

Let us suppose your boyfriend is very much into going to the gym. He believes in fitness and his food habits are rigid. He constantly reminds you what to eat and how long you should exercise. When you visit his family, his mother also verbalizes, ad nauseam, about the correct foods to consume.

She reminds you how skinny she was in college and remarks about her weight constantly. You have heard at least one hundred times that at your age she exercised at the gym twice a day. She gives an opinion about your clothes: how one piece of clothing either tends to make you look smaller or larger. You wonder will her remarks will ever end.

Some people have an obsession about body issues. This mother and son may not even know the depths of their obsessions. And it is not your place to fix a problem. All you can do is honor yourself.

Example 4: Psychological Obsession

Keri's husband, Lawrence, broke his hip riding his horse. Due to complications, he had to convalesce for three months. After three weeks, he was able to move around the house. With time on his hands, the computer became his new friend. He joined the cyber world of chat rooms and computer games.

Soon he began obsessing. When his wife and children came home, he hardly acknowledged them with a hello and he rarely stopped what he was doing. If his children interrupted him, he became angry. Sometimes he was severe—downright nasty.

After a particularly mean incident, Kerri put her foot down. Lawrence promised he would alter his behavior. But within a few days he was back fixating on cyber space. Keri was about to wash her hands of her marriage. She told Lawrence he had to make some serious changes or their marriage was over. They went to a psychoanalyst.

Lawrence made an effort to shake his old ways. He placed the computer in his brother's home until he could wean himself off of his obsession. And by making a serious effort, Keri and her family are now doing well.

Example 5: Psychological Pain and Suffering

Let us suppose your best friend explains to you that she cannot invite you to her son's small wedding because of limited space. In the meantime, you discovered she invited a mutual acquaintance.

A multitude of feelings stir in your mind and heart. You feel forsaken and sad. All these years you thought you had a close relationship. You contemplate confronting your friend to ask her why she invited the other person to the wedding and left you out. You want to express how upset you feel.

If you go that route, I am sure she will give you an excellent reason to cradle your illusion. Who knows, you may gain a certain satisfaction by challenging the issue. Regardless, you are going to have to bite the bullet and face what is. Be grateful that your friend shattered your illusion.

Example 6: Psychological Pain and Misunderstanding

Imagine that at the beginning of the year your partner promised to take you on a special vacation—your choice. You looked forward to the trip and labored to make a memorable itinerary. Two weeks before the vacation, your partner told you he changed his mind. He explained he would rather go camping and fishing with his buddies.

You mentioned you have been looking forward to the trip and spending, much needed, quality time together. He reciprocated by suggesting you invite a friend to take his place. Psychologically, you want to rehash your problem with anyone who will listen. When you speak of your disappointment, the ache in your heart subsides (your ego is being occupied).

This situation should not have gone this far. Were you listening to each other, especially when you were commenting on the vacation's itinerary? What was your partner's reaction? Did he mention he preferred camping, but you decided to plan for something else?

Complaining or arguing about the matter will not do either of you any good—try honest dialogue. This is a subject both you and your partner will have to work out together. Keep blame out of the equation.

Find clarity. A relationship cannot be based on the illusions of what you would like it to be. Disappointments from illusions always cause one to live in psychological pain.

Example 7: Psychological Pain, Disappointment

You and your best friend, Terry, did everything together. You talked on the telephone, double dated, shopped, and told each other intimate secrets. Out of the blue, Terry betrayed your trust. She discussed confidential information with a mutual acquaintance. You feel humiliated and heart broken.

You confronted Terry and reminded her that you never divulged one of her secrets to anyone. Terry laughed and replied that you were making a big deal out of nothing. Her sassy attitude completely caught you off guard. You do not understand why Terry no longer gives you support. A part of you wishes you could make everything different. You want to move forward, but it seems impossible. You wonder how you will be able to trust anyone again.

Your mind twirls in circles. You blame yourself for being too trusting. You blame your friend for being cavalier. Nothing seems to relieve your gut-wrenching pain. You think of revenge. Your ego whispers you could reveal one of Terry's juiciest secrets.

If you did disclose one of her secrets, it would not bring your friendship back nor would this action help you to heal. You need to adjust to this unpleasant situation. Face the fact of "what is." Cry. Actually, a good cry helps one grieve through a situation and speeds the transition. Talk to a friend. Concentrate on a hobby. Do what you love to do best. Use your imagination to create an experience that works for you. By making a conscious effort to open your energy field, you eventually find the peace you seek.

Example 8: Psychological Pain, Change

At the age of fifteen, Joyce's daughter, Megan began to date. Megan's dating was particularly tough on Joyce. She did not like her little girl maturing. She felt sad she was no longer Megan's focal point. And as Megan's hormones took the lead, her strong independent streak became more pronounced. Joyce convinced herself that Megan's actions and decisions were foolish and erratic. Joyce's disposition clouded the days with complacency and worry. She wondered if Megan's perplexing teenage days would ever show clarity.

To find balance, Joyce needs to give full attention to her unsettling experience. This new passage in her mother/daughter relationship deserves honesty. Heartfelt dialogues will keep their relationship alive. When Joyce expresses her own vulnerability, it will demonstrate to Megan that her mother has faith in her—lifting their relationship to a higher level.

Parents, do not allow your child to live in limbo—relate. There is nothing as complicated or as invigorating than growing into a young adult. Add to your child's magical and mysterious years.

Even when you feel frustrated, rejoice in the never-ending pursuit of parenting and the intimacy parenting entails. If you feel you are suffering through the process of parenting, remember suffering is caused by a psychological thought pattern. In reality, before you know it, both of you will be ten years older looking back on these hazy days.

All any parent can do is teach their child to take responsibility. One must live in the moment, understand his or her actions and exercise compassion. Above all, do not give in to fearful sensations. They will lead you down an egotistical road.

Be open and notice if your child is experiencing sweet or bitter relationships. What are his or her thought patterns and actions? The gratification your son or daughter shows on the outside will be the union they are experiencing on the inside.

If you sincerely feel someone is harming your child, you have a right to put your foot down, but do not expect it to be an easy task. Most children, especially during the puberty years, feel any type of constructive criticism is just plain criticizing (see Chapter XVII, "Criticism and Constructive Criticism"). If by chance, your child refuses to listen, take the high road, pick your battles wisely, or maybe look to a third party could to guide you both toward harmony.

Example 9: Psychological Pain, Recognition

Lance lived a privileged existence and his parents indulged his every whim. He went to the finest schools and traveled worldwide. After graduating from college, Lance set his sights on a dream career. He knew just how his life should present itself. He felt he deserved the highest salary and the public arena should recognize his excellent qualifications—immediately.

For two years Lance bounced from employer to employer. He would not embarrass himself staying in a position that did not give him the recognition he deserved. His last employer asked him to resign. Lance felt he had been given a bad deal. Why should he have to prove himself when everyone around him was so incompetent?

By playing the psychological head game, Lance fooled himself. If he put as much effort into being forthright, using his insight, and listening to others he would have had all the recognition he deserves. Throughout life everyone has to fight against his or her psychological bumps and be cognitive of what the present moment truly offers.

Example 10: Psychological Pain, Behavior Patterns

The school years can be a bit distressing for most children. It is important parents or guardians show children they have a responsibility in all relationships. Also, keep in mind children are not always aware of the connection between their behavior and how they treat others. That is why it is so important to keep an open dialogue.

Exercise:

Try this example. Concentrate on a past experience. Observe how alive this experience resides in your mind; how it makes a situation seem real. Once your feeling triggers a reaction—you become hooked on the impression of the event to justify your psychological sensation—keeping you in a stuck mode.

Note a real feeling has a forward movement—an energy—where chronological time stands still. You are not in the past or projecting the future; your priorities do not go askew.

Questions:

Have you often pushed for something for so long that you have forgotten why you actually wanted it? Do you allow the painful moments from the past to consume your life? Do you heap your struggles in a rigid pile, and somehow expect someone or something to relieve you from the pain of those experiences?

• Free yourself by living in the present moment, joyfully.

GRIEF

Intellectually, we know all things pass and losing a loved one is one of the many processes connected to our ever-shifting world. To help yourself heal, make a point to become observant. Note that it takes time for one's heart to mend and to assimilate the grief and sadness in one's reality.

Also, the art of healing wears many faces. Be open. A healing could come from an individual's kind words, nurture, your higher self, or by practicing a particular ritual.

Example: Grief

Marsha was crushed when her grandmother passed away. She felt as though a knife had pierced her heart. Her sadness reached inside a dark place until she made a pact with herself. She would no longer become close to an elderly person again. Marsha thought she could control her feelings by closing her heart. She failed to realize each person who enters her life adds another dimension to her character.

Her ego wants everything to be as it was—impossible for nothing stays the same. Marsha must go through a grieving process and realize time cannot wipe her emptiness away. Part of her heart will be with her grandmother forever. All any of us can do is honor our loved ones and begin living the life we have been given.

PART III
STUMBLING BLOCKS

FORGIVENESS

Delving into my mind
I lay awake thinking of my mistake
A synchronistic event
I can't rationalize what I have done
I'm not trying too
I don't even know myself
Maybe it was our arguments
The way you looked at me
A misinformation
That froze a crust of ice around my heart
Until...
I could not define my existence
Or grasp the edges of my space
Or walk with my head held high
I lost the joyful dance
An essence

Now that our path is broken
I reach out to you with an open heart
My heart in hand
Hopeful - Hoping
You'll understand

Can we pass through the state of forgiveness
Without blame?
Is it possible to transform our gentle spirits
To a place of trust?
To a place brimming with love?
You tell me
I'm waiting.

CHAPTER XIII

Making critical decisions and taking them to creative solutions diminishes turbulent traps.

EMOTIONS

Our subjective viewpoints place us in an emotional state until our judgments become hazy. It does not matter if we are having an emotional high or an emotional low. There is incompleteness in our existence when we do not understand the root connected to our emotions.

We get into trouble when we project our distorted emotions onto others. This attitude breeds isolation and it is unnatural. Examine your emotions in the present moment. Your loved ones will be glad you did.

Questions:

Do you allow you emotions to get the best of you? Are you flexible? How do you overcome adversity?

• Truly loving someone encourages and does not demand.

MEASURING YOURSELF AGAINST OTHERS

When people put on airs, they are essentially disguising their misery. Note the people in your life who use their material possessions, knowledge, or education to show their superiority? They are similar to the donkey with a carrot in front of its head. The donkey chases the carrot to the point of exhaustion—never receiving satisfaction. Possessions are what they are, just possessions. Likewise, the prestige of a particular profession—as with everything in life—is a personal experience. It is a part of you but not all of you.

Another form of measurement is the representation of an individual's IQ. Realize if a person has a high IQ and happens to be beautiful or handsome, it is their birth gene pool characteristic. Whatever resource, talent, or genius one has inherited, it is just that. In many ways, we are as different from each other as the vegetables are in a tossed salad. For balance, there needs to be a variety of people in the world. Therefore, each person should be grateful for his or her own distinctive individuality.

Life would be rewarding if individuals could experience the same simplicity as the changing seasons. The seasons do not have a beginning or ending. They flow whether we have an exceptional day or a tragedy—the sun still shines and the rain still falls. Life has the same continuing process.

The ego's flawed mechanism pushes one into believing someone else is having a better life. End this daft presumption that you are not measuring up or that you are somehow better than someone else.

Take whatever problem you think you have and hold your judgments. Your subjective views are words and deeds tied in the knot of expectation. Search for commonalities;

they will trump your differences. Bring meaning to your life. Treat each moment as the most precious item you can own and live it as if it were your last.

Example: Measurement

I have a friend who worries about her appearance. She constantly measures herself again other women. It is always something. Her skin is not smooth enough, she has wrinkles, her stomach is not flat, and her thighs are too large. She has had extensive surgery and she still complains about her flaws.

It is natural to compare our bodies to others, but if we are metally clear, we realize that one's so-called flaws are not flaws at all; they are our unique differences. Think about it: our spirits are one of a kind and so are our bodies. Dare to be yourself, and enjoy all the qualities your body contains.

Exercise:
Dismantle your tunnel vision and open yourself to endless possibilities (see Chapter XIX Meditation Exercises).

INSECURITY

From a distance, some individuals may look as though they are contented with their lives, but they keep their true characters masked from others. Usually these individuals cannot form strong relationships. They occupy their time with busyness to make sure they do not have any spare time to think or feel. They neither listen nor experience anything. They lump all their relationships together while their energy weakens and their insecurity deepens.

A little insecurity is okay. It demonstrates one has new, unexplored grounds to cover. But the insecurity that makes individuals feel they are less than they are needs to be addressed. If individuals are insecure about their physical appearance, lack of education, or financial status, they are dividing themselves—reaffirming the insecurity until it owns them.

To break insecurity's hold on you, ask why you feel insecure. Why are you measuring yourself against others? Speak to others about your insecurity. The more you vocalize your insecurity the less insecure you are going to feel.

Giving in to peer pressure is another sign of insecurity. As soon as individuals react to please others, they are actors performing in a relationship. They cannot experience their true selves and they are separating themselves from self-love—the link that connects us to one another.

Example: Insecurity

Throughout Judy's childhood, she was overweight. At one point, her parents took her to a nutritionist/dietitian counselor. They had hoped a healthy diet with specific rules would guide Judy to change her bingeing habit. Her dieting days and months turned into years with her weight fluctuating from twenty pounds gained to twenty pounds lost. At her high school graduation, she vowed she was through with dieting.

She said, "I am fat. I will never look like most women and I accept who I am. I may not have much of a social life, but I can concentrate on making an academic standing."

Years later Judy graduated in the top fivepercent of her class. She did not have a problem getting a prestigious position in the business world, but secretly she felt like a failure. She sensed she needed a new outlook.

She spoke to her best friend, Libby, mentioning she was dissatisfied with her appearance. Libby suggested since diets did not seem to help, why not try altering her appearance. Judy could purchase distinctive clothes; change her hair style, wear makeup, and most of all accept in her heart that she is a remarkable person.

Sometimes when a person consciously reshuffles his or her appearance on the outside it transforms something from within. Allow your spirit to shine. Listen to those who love you, he or she may give you an insight that leads you toward a fulfilling path.

Questions:

Are you afraid to express yourself? Are you the type of person who will go to any length to be accepted? Do you live in your mind? Do you allow fear or insecurities to guide your heart?

• Learn to let go of the mindset of proving yourself. Do not allow people to subtly or blatantly devalue your worth. Realize it is your responsibility to shape your days into a healthy atmosphere.

Unfairness and Resentment

No one is capable of controlling the unfairness in the world; under most circumstances, we can only do our best. And how we look at certain circumstances can make a difference in the quality of our lives. For the most part, try to be thankful for life's eruptions. They give us the chance to think from a new vantage point, change, and—best yet—to feel.

Example 1: Unfairness and Resentment

Todd worked at the same company for six years. Through the years he has been rewarded for his services with an ample salary increase. He thoroughly enjoyed his career and working with his friendly coworkers made the day fly.

Todd's world changed the day he had a genius idea that would make the department run more efficiently. Todd relayed his idea to his supervisor, Joe. Joe took the credit for Todd's idea. He not only received special acknowledgement, but also received a substantial raise. Needless to say, Todd felt mistreated.

One evening when Joe and Todd worked overtime, Todd confronted Joe about his betrayal. To Todd's surprise, Joe looked him square in the eye, and with a waterfall of words denied that he had anything to do with his idea.

Todd left his office fuming. He mulled the conversation over in his mind—continuously. He was consumed by the thoughts of what could have been. Todd resents Joe's attitude and how the company recognized him. Almost every day he chatters about Joe to his co-workers. Daily, he makes idle threats about quitting his job.

Most of his coworkers sympathize with his plight. They either give him an affectionate pat him on the back or show him a sad understanding look. Todd feels defeated. He hates every minuscule minute he sees Joe. Worse yet, he is falling behind on his work.

Todd has a choice to gain wisdom from his experience. He can remain bitter or push his ego aside. The fact remains whether he keeps his position, transfers within the company, or resigns he cannot change what is. Todd is a creative person. In the future, he is bound to think of another fantastic idea. He has learned his lesson. From now on he shall document all his creative thoughts.

In essence, when a misfortune consumes you with thoughts of what could have been, realize you will bleed away the present moment and miss the experiences that will turn your life around.

Example 2: Unfairness and Deception

Louise has a chance to go to a special event with her cousin Jane. Jane told Louise to wear something casual. She reiterated, do not wear a fancy dress or a skirt; jeans are fine.

Louise's mother dropped her at the destination. To her dismay, the event was a semi-formal—she was under-dressed. She could not believe her cousin would purposely mislead her.

Louise thought to herself, maybe I should call my mother and ask her to take me home, complain to Jane—as if that would do any good—or forget what I am wearing and just be myself. Louise decided to let go of the situation and have fun with her experience.

Louise now has an awareness of her cousin's true character. And from this moment on, she will recheck her cousin's information—twice.

Questions:

Do you feel the world does not treat you fairly? Do you retaliate against individuals you think have wronged you?

• Feelings of resentment or unfairness tend to magnify one's aloneness further—blocking any chance at happiness.

Chapter XIV

Persnickety mood swings need careful observation.

Stuck in Negative Patterns

As I mentioned before, when we have been victims of an upsetting circumstance, our injuries keep us in an eternal shallowness mixed with multiple sensations. We either show our defeat outright or hide behind a façade. Our egos make us feel like losers by reminding us of a gloomy situation. Living in an ongoing circle of misery, we feel isolated and do not know how to draw a respectful boundary around ourselves or others.

Everyone has a chance to be more than they initially thought they could be. Think of life as giant elastic stretching to and fro. The elastic is pliable, but when the elastic stretches beyond its limit, there is a good chance it will break. However, if the elastic is stretched slowly with care there is a good chance it will extend beyond its normal capacity. By moving forward we stretch ourselves. We accomplish longevity—substance. Yet we must always rest and go back to the beginning to relax into our original shape. We are who we are and—by understanding our infinite—we embrace our strengths and our limitations.

It is better to squeeze the best out of a day and enjoy all situations than feel bewildered and exasperated by what we thought could have been. By expanding our spiritual freedom, we are empowered. That is why we should always reflect on our actions—there are days we will be accountable for them.

Questions:

Do you allow the pressure of the modern world to strangle you? Do you obsess about something that you cannot change? Do you dwell on regret?

•Do not allow your ego to be your keeper.

TEMPTATION

Temptation is ego-based and motivated by instant gratification. To be wise in the face of temptation, honestly ask yourself why are you vulnerable to the lure of a quick high? Why am I doing something that is so different from what I need?"

Change the path you are on. Invest in a rich full life by living in the moment, find joy in your relationships, educate yourself, or take up a new hobby. Today, connect to humanity's wonder.

DESIRE

The definition of desire: A wish, a craving for urgent gratification, a desperate yearning, a feeling that one lacks something or a profound need to make one's life feel fulfilled. The desire convinces a person their wantonness is special.

Desire needs to feed itself to stay alive. Note the ego is guiding you when you have an overwhelming urge to make decisions on what feels good in a weak moment, instead of making a decision based on something steadfast. Under this circumstance, one will never feel grounded or satisfied. Soon individuals become hypnotized and caught in a paradox to justify their desire. Do not indulge a desire without reflecting. Always ask if your actions are hurting someone.

Envy

Why do people rarely envy strangers but easily envy those close to them, such as a family member, friend, or coworker? We may envy someone's lucky break, although many of us would not want the shadows connected to another person's life. On the other side of the coin, it seems people are never happy with what they have. They usually want what they thought they had in the past or hope that future events will take them out of their misery.

Envy is your ego whispering you have not measured up to an expectation. Do not allow envy to weigh you down. Observe how your thoughts fuel envy and keep you melancholy. Break the back of envy; acknowledge the successes and the joys of others. This action will liberate you from your ego.

Addictions

The definition of addiction: a practice or pursuit through overuse. The public recognizes there are many forms of addiction. To name a few: drinking, smoking, gambling, excessive spending, sexual promiscuity, and eating disorders. Also, some people are addicted to being a know-it-all, watching television, playing video games, or obsessing with cyberspace.

Addictions begin from the bottom of one's psyche. If someone has gone through some type of traumatic incident, (see Chapter III, "Traumatic Change") they may self medicate—hoping to end their pain. Their tradeoff is living in a senseless limbo—alone and barren.

Physically abusing someone is another form of addiction. When perpetrators' lives are empty and out of control, they focus on controlling others. Hearing someone screaming or pleading gives them a sense of power, although momentary. This power is similar to a drug high.

After the incident, they usually ask for forgiveness (another power play). But their violence must escalate. For their new high needs the element of surprise to retain its power—further deadening one's spirit. At this juncture, they have closed the ability to move forward and some type of intervention is needed.

However, one cannot force anyone into making changes. No amount of love, begging, withdrawal, punishment, or crying can make a difference. Unfortunately, there are no deal breakers. And sometimes pressuring a person could make matters worse. One has to take a step toward change for his or her own salvation. I suggest anyone who has an addicted loved one visit Al-Anon. This organization helps individuals to understand the addict's persona and the challenges they will be facing in his or her relationship.

GUILT

Wikipedia's definition of guilt: Guilt is the state of having committed an offense, crime, violation, wrong, or the feeling of responsibility or remorse for some offense, crime, etc., whether real or imagined.

After making a mistake, most of us feel guilty. If indeed there was a mistake, own it—apologize. Question if you are keeping your psychological guilt feelings alive. This is my guilt buster. Never delay an awkward moment. If necessary, make a compromise and happily do so.

Example 1: Guilt and Illness

Let us suppose a longtime friend—someone who helped you in the past—is currently in the midst of the blues. She rejects your invitations and ignores your telephone calls. When she does speak to you, she wallows in self-pity repeating the same monologue—"woe is me." And she refuses to take advice.

You have had it with her excuses, and as far as you are concerned, her therapist is not helping her either. You want to give up, but a tremendous guilt feeling envelopes you. You feel guilty about leaving your friend in the lurch.

Not every friendship survives life's challenges, and not every friend can come to one's rescue. Question yourself through and through. Do you accept your friend's place in life—regardless of the hard work involved or would you rather move on? Make a decision—hence guilt disappears.

Example 2: Guilt and Relationship

I know a couple who has lived together for ten years—the last five years they have been engaged. The groom hesitated to rush into matrimony. Finally, the wedding date was set. As the bride planned her wedding, she thought about her commitment. She realized that she no longer loves or is interested in marrying her fiancé. She is contemplating calling off the relationship. Yet she feels guilty wasting all those years. She does not know what to do. She hates the thought of disappointing her family and friends.

For years the bride lived in a comfort zone. She never bothered to question the depth of her relationship. She was fixated on the idea of marriage. Once her wish came to fruition, she started to focus on what is. Her guilt comes from distress of change and hating herself for making an error in judgment.

She needs to free herself. Admit she is no longer in love with her man. I believe if one does what is absolutely right for oneself—selflessly—his or her actions will be right for others.

Example 3: Guilt and Neighbor

Olivia lives in an upscale condo neighborhood where animals are not allowed to roam. Unfortunately, she is having a problem with a neighbor's cat. The cat continuously relieves itself in her yard. She mentioned to her neighbor— as amiably as possible—she would like her to keep her cat out of her yard. The neighbor replied, "Cats tend to roam." She waited two weeks. Nothing changed.

Olivia feels guilty about going to the condo association to complain. She does not want to cause trouble. But since her neighbor is uncooperative she has no place to turn. By bringing a problem to the surface, my friend should not feel she is creating ill will. Think, when someone has enough nerve to do something they are not supposed to do, the rest of us have the right to speak-up.

Chapter XV

Celebrate your successes no matter how small.

Unfulfilled People

Unfulfilled people become spiritless hungry ghosts who feed off the unhappiness of others. They seek victims to satisfy their insatiable appetite. Think of the hungry ghost as an entity with a gigantic body and small mouth. It perpetually feels empty—never at peace. Their approach to a victim is subtle. Every word and situation is carefully chosen to manipulate individuals into the idea they are not worthy.

Soon your sense of self crumbles, destroying your clarity. Physically and psychologically you become submerged in self doubt. The present moment feels wearying and stultifying. You hate yourself as well as others. At this juncture, you are willing to listen to a hungry ghost's empty promises. You become a hungry ghost. Now you are prepared to pull others into your solitary dead zone.

How does one break free from being a hungry ghost? Starvation is the key. Examine your motives. Be mindful of your actions—own your responsibilities. Recognize that it is okay to make a mistake. Keep your emotions intact. Express yourself with compassion. Do not allow your paranoia to get the best of you. Every time you feel yourself slipping back into the hungry ghost syndrome, free yourself by speaking the truth.

Example: Hungry Ghost Syndrome
1. Gossiping:
A person hides insecurities by diverting his or her inadequacy toward others.
2. Immaturity, Feeling substandard:
Anyone taking foolish chances such as drinking and driving, sexual promiscuity, and anger are not being responsible for his or her actions.
3. Fear of intimacy, Violence:
A person is emotionally tormented or in psychological pain.
4. Demanding, Obnoxious, Rambling, Cursing:
Individuals live in a world of delusion and illusions.
5. Lying and Cheating:
Feeling bewildered—at a loss. Hate in one's heart.
6. Spending Money Irrationally:
Measuring one's worth through others—not feeling good enough.
7. Avoiding Responsibility:
Peter Pan syndrome: Not wanting to grow up.

Example: Hungry Ghost
How many people have you heard give a compliment, but at the same time take something away? For example, many years ago I worked in an office where there was a young lady who dressed in her own style—her look be-

longed to her. Many of the colleagues—behind her back—criticized her appearance. Some of them felt they should approach her with the advice she would be very attractive "only if" she knew how to dress correctly.

It is this sort of condescending remark that is really an insult fancied up as a compliment. Note that hungry ghosts seek to ridicule someone in order to feel superior. If individuals are truly happy with themselves, they would not want to change another person.

Exercise:

Take a deep breath. Say out loud, "I breathe in the positive." As you exhale, say out loud "I release myself from... (state the negative situation) and I choose to move forward." Practice this step whenever you feel aggravated or you are in a blaming mode.

ARGUMENTS

Most arguments are based on two people seeing the opposite side of a concept. Points are weighed by subjective facts and internalized by the ego's meticulous score. A difference of opinion cannot be resolved where one stands with his or her feet firmly planted into the ground.

If it is imperative to give an opinion, try explaining the positive basis of your evidence. People are more likely to adopt new ideas than drop an old ones. And they are apt to be receptive to well-grounded comments when they are not annoyed. In all discussions, there are no easy answers—usually the answer lies between the best sides of a choice.

How necessary is it to expose a person's weakness or belief? I cannot think of anyone who would not balk at being singled out because he or she is wrong. This behavior provokes defensiveness. Besides, showing people the error of their ways does not make someone right—an opinion is an opinion. Note that there are moments in life one should stay mum, especially if the subject is none of anyone's business.

INTIMIDATION AND MANIPULATION

Some people use clever criticism to gloss the truth of a subject. They know how to rationalize and extract the truth from reality to assure an upper hand. This type of behavior tilts the balance in our relationships. Learn to listen to the uncomfortable noises surrounding your energy field (see Chapter I, "How to Nurture Your Energy Field"). The noises are showing you that some type of negative pattern is forming.

Empathetically be smart. This is a time to question your involvement. See a relationship for what it is, and then make a decision according to your reality. You have the right to sit at home, leave town, or make plans that may not coincide with anyone else's wishes.

Example 1: Intimidation and Manipulation, Living in a Shadow

Julian lives in his father's shadow. His father's dynamic personality and witty charm topped with a silver tongue makes him a force to be reckoned with. No one could talk anyone into anything or defuse torrid situations quite like he. As far back as Julian could remember, his father primed him to be part of the family business. Julian felt there would not be any other place in this world he would rather be.

In an impromptu moment—after graduating from college—Julian's best friend Bob asked him to join him on a summer trip to Europe with their three roommates. Their trip would be their last hurrah before they started their careers.

On the trip, the young men related to each other profoundly. They conversed about where their lives were headed and their dreams. Bob mentioned he was looking forward to his career. He could not hold back his enthusiasm. The rest of his friends felt the same. That evening their candid conversations started Julian thinking.

The next day at breakfast Julian divulged he was not sure he wanted to run his father's business. It was not that he hated the thought. He just realized last night it might not be for him. Bob asked him if he had a career preference.

Without hesitating, he said, "I would rather teach business than become a part of it. I already have my master's degree in business. I could ask my uncle, who is a professor at the local college, to direct me. But now that I made up my mind, I'm worried about my father's reaction."

He mimicked his father's mannerism, "Julian listen! I won't have this. You're going to work with me. That's the way it's supposed to be. Let's think this out. Work for the company one year. If you do not like it, then you can quit. Do not turn your back on me. Give me one year!"

His tone changed as his voiced choked, "Dad has such a strong personality. Suppose I give into his wishes. I shall hate myself for the rest of my life."

Julian is in conflict. He wants to do what is right for him, but he also does not want to disappoint his father. The reality of the situation: Julian cannot control how his father feels anymore than his father can control how he feels.

After his father absorbs the shock of change, Julian and his father can start from a new beginning—two men choosing their place in life. Through love and acceptance, they will find a connection—a place filled with joy.

Example 2: Intimidation and Manipulation, Hostility

Let us suppose your co-worker, Buddy, took the liberty of helping himself to your office supplies. Sometimes he even sits at your desk and makes telephone calls while you stand there fuming. Also, he thinks nothing of rearranging the articles you have on your desk top. Once he even re-arranged your files.

You told him gently to leave your supplies alone and not to sit at your desk. With a surprised look on his face, he snaps, "Why are you overreacting? What is the big deal? No one else seems to mind me sitting at their desks."

You cannot be soft with this type of person. He needs a direct and firm approach. Buddy may act friendly, but he is definitely hostile and aggressive. Tell him outright he is not permitted to touch anything on your desk. And if he persists in this behavior, you will report him to the office manager.

Example 3: Intimidation and Manipulation, Self Preservation

For the past four years your nephew visited and stayed at your Boston apartment for a week. You enjoyed his visit even though it was a little cramped—he slept on the living room sofa.

Moving ahead, he is married and now has twins. He notified you he would be visiting with his family in a month. And he plans on staying in your apartment. You explained to him you would be happy to see everyone, but your apartment is too small to accommodate his family. You firmly suggested he stay at the local hotel.

For your own self preservation, you had to take a stand. There is a difference between putting out the doormat or being one. Pushy people have no qualms about shoving others to the limit. Make yourself clear. You have a right to your own space. The pushy person either understands or he or she does not.

GOSSIP

If you feel the need to gossip, you are looking to relieve some sort of psychological pain—a temporary solution. And by diverting your misery to gossiping you are simply entertaining your own dullness.

How do you stop yourself from gossiping? Ask your spirit to release you from the past. You will receive an epiphany. Be prepared, your ego will resist.

Questions:

Do you gossip? Do you make it a point to gossip against those who you think have slighted you? Do you repeat rumors about the private affairs of others?

• Bring comfort to anyone who needs it.

VENTING

I advise everyone to vent; everyone needs a sounding board. For a word or a deed held back is as ineffectual to harmony as words said in anger. Venting is different from gossiping. As you communicate, there is honesty. You are not defaming anyone. There is a sense of relaxed freedom.

One's significant other or close friends should be able to listen to complaints about life's ups and downs with empathy. In addition, always honor the person who has lent you an ear.

GREED

Greed has a magical elusive allure that lies dormant in everyone. A greedy person fulfills one accomplishment, to serve the self (ego). Greed justifies one's action with a multitude of excuses—destroying one's balance and breaking the present moment into fragmented pieces. This harmful action will isolate you and keep you from connecting to all things.

Example: Greed

Vivian is a server. She has been with the same restaurant for years. Recently Vivian has been having financial difficulties. Her husband lost his job. Shortly thereafter, he gained employment, but at a substantial pay reduction. In the meantime, the manager of the restaurant hired two servers; Vivian was aware she would not be receiving as many tips. Needless to say, she was upset.

As the new servers worked longer hours and had regular customers, they noticed on particular shifts their regular customers were only leaving a dollar or two in tips. When the servers put their heads together, they realized the tips were sparse whenever Vivian was on their shift. The head server, Susie, saw Vivian walk by the new server's tables. She nonchalantly slipped most of the tips in her apron pocket.

Susie had an idea. After customers left the tips on the tables, waitresses took turns putting a red mark in the corner of each bill. After lunch, around two o'clock, the manager called Vivian into his office and asked her to empty her apron in front of the servers. Sure enough, Vivian had red-tipped money in her possession.

Even though she was caught stealing, Vivian denied the allegations. The other servers refused to work with her. The company transferred her to another branch, and she was warned to behave herself. The following month she repeated her habit and was fired.

Vivian felt she deserved taking someone else's tips. After all, she was down and out. She never considered that the other servers needed their tips as much as she.

Good Luck/Bad Luck

Let us question is there a phenomena called good luck or bad luck? Think why is it when a happy event occurs we chalk it up to good luck. Or when something irritating occurs we call it bad luck.

One cannot strive for good luck because the phenomenon of luck happens without a history or a future. If a person had a plan and the plan is workable, it is considered good luck. Struggles in life have nothing to do with luck. They are experiences.

Good luck is similar to grace happening to you, not because of you. It is the telephone call full of reverence—just when you needed a lift. It is a friend sharing his or her life with you. It is getting up in the morning and realizing you have the day in front of you. Your good luck could be a dream come true but with much hard work behind it.

Bad luck is the phenomena joining with other polarities in life that bring something to a climax. For example if you had an accident, loss of employment, a loved one deserted you, or you had a health problem you would automatically consider those things bad luck.

Think of an abrupt circumstance as a "do-over" not an ending. Besides, and unforeseen circumstance forces you to check your priorities—similar to challenges. It gives you an "aha" moment—bringing you to a different mode of thinking. Maybe that is what some would call a sign of good luck.

Chapter XVI

*It is okay to explore one's needs
and cater to them abundantly.*

Reality

The word reality means there is a fact or quality that something is real. For example, it is a reality a person has brown eyes. It is a reality someone has a 160 IQ. It is a reality someone is artistically talented. We measure our mundane world with this type of reality.

And it is in this place where the marvelous, the ordinary, and the surreal coexist.

Examples: Life's Realities

1. Healthy or Disabled

Some people are born healthy. Others may have a physical or psychological handicap while others may have excellent health, but later have an accident or a disease that makes them incapacitated

2. High or Low IQs

Some individuals have a high IQ and achieve their goals. Others with a high IQ may hardly get by. On the other hand, some people with an average IQ may forge ahead gaining a revered place in the world.

3. Financial Resources

For the majority of people, their financial resources fluctuate. Other individuals will not be able to spend their resources in a lifetime while some only have a fraction of bare necessities.

4. Ultimate Reality

The way we perceive the world is a personal reality—one's belief. When we truly treasure our reality/belief for the life substance it gives, it is impossible to destroy anyone else's reality. At this juncture, we become part of an ultimate reality—a blending of many possibilities.

Follow Your Truth

Truth has nothing to do with a belief or an opinion. It is a clarity where one is free of illusions. Imagine truth as a highway; it is stationary. Truth does not change. The transportation (bus) is your personal reality—changing as you perceive life differently. How you use your transportation to get to your destination is a choice. If you try to separate the truth (what is) from your reality, you may awaken the hungry ghost.

Selfless Choices

Everyone has heard of Mother Teresa. She followed her reality and dedicated her life to the poor in India. Through her act of selflessness, she provided much time and energy to those who were less fortunate. Her life-long dedication, a personal choice, connects her to an unspoken joy.

Some religions may say this unspoken joy is God. Others may say that joy is a grace that binds humanity together. Whether altruistic or self-absorbed all individuals are destined to make choices in accordance to his or her personal parameter. It is in this place he or she will reap rewards or live with despair.

WHAT IS THE PURPOSE OF LIFE?

Through the centuries many philosophers have written about the meaning of life. And we still ask… is there a purpose to life? Are we part of a God? Is there a worldly intelligence far beyond our grasp? Whatever our speculation, it is just that. The only thing I am sure of is we are connected to the moment and each other.

RELIGIOUS BELIEFS

Everyone tends to socialize with those who give them comfort. This common thread binds us together and our religious practice cinches that solace. A priest, rabbi, minister, guru, politician, or any person with a powerful influence over the media can teach an idea. However, it takes a lifetime for individuals to understand and practice their spiritual path

Christ led his life showing others a diversified mode of thinking. He listened to his God, and followed a creed different from his time. Christ's reality and his insights were his life's experiences. His spiritual quest belonged to him. Others may choose to follow or dismiss his teachings.

Buddha was another man whose reputation gave him credence. Through most standards, Buddha had everything in life—a wife, son, wealth, and health. But he felt there was more to life than the standard material and social comforts he enjoyed, and left his life behind him.

After years of wandering the country, contemplating, and living as a beggar he came to a conclusion. Life is filled with suffering, although humans can alleviate suffering by overcoming ignorance and leading a moral life. Through the practice of meditation, Buddhists believe we learn to let go of our attachments and reduce our suffering.

They also believe that Bodhisattvas walk among us, a person who has achieved great moral and spiritual wisdom, but rejects nirvana (blissfulness) and reincarnates—often—to guide others toward enlightenment. I think there are many people in the world who are Bodhisattvas. They teach and show us the joy connected to kindness and compassion.

Here are a few magnanimous leaders, who have followed their spirit and shared their wisdom, insights, and teachings: Whitman, Emerson, Thoreau, Gandhi, Arthur Schopenhauer, Chasam Sofer, Carl Sagan, Louis Pasteur, Plato, Benazir Bhutto, and Pythagoras. Again, we may follow their teachings, but their energy fields (individuality) cannot be duplicated. If we think so, we are living an illusion.

CONNECTING TO YOUR ANCESTORS

Another form of religion is Spiritualism. Spiritualists (mediums) believe when a loved one passes to the next world he or she will help a family member or friend with life's obstacles.

A medium interprets the information of the spirit's message through symbols, visualizations, or words. Just like with all religious leaders a medium would not tell anyone to mistreat someone, ask for money to give their blessing or lift a curse. They guide and believe the actions one takes in a given situation should be handled with compassion. And no one should be an emotional extortionist to anybody.

KARMA

Karma is a Hindu word from Sanskrit: it means action. The stem word, karman, is derived from the root verb (dhAtu) kRRi, to do—doing. Traditionally speaking karma is the successive state of an action, which determines the faith of another action. Individuals experience this natural condition daily. The familiar term is cause and effect—a polarity.

Our motives produce an action and the action becomes the cause. Karma has its own mysterious schedule by dispensing karmic justice with impunity. You cannot save someone from their karma or prevent a person from making a gross mistake. Whether your actions are contributing to a cause of pleasure or pain, your experience belongs to you, as someone else's karma belongs to them. There is only one way to go through a karmic experience— by oneself.

Many people believe we arrive in this world with karmic scars or we accumulate karma by "doing." I feel everyone has a choice to liberate themselves from a karmic (past) experience by simply living in the present moment. We also decide how we perceive the world and how we use our free will. Simply put, confront choices and allow insights to flow.

Ultimately, whether you believe in karma or not, you can deliver yourself to your best potential. Always question what you are "doing" with your life RIGHT NOW.

Example 1: Karma, Childhood

Connie was born a cheerful child. She automatically looked at a problem from two sides. She could see the sun shining behind every gray cloud. Everyone liked her; she was incredibly popular. As she grew older, people opened-up to her warmth. A girlfriend gave her designer clothes, she was invited on trips, and a distant relative paid her tuition to a private school.

At sixteen, her parent made her drop out of the private school. They found her a job where she worked one evening a week and weekends. Weekly, she handed her paycheck to her father. Connie did not question her parent's decision. She thought after her family's resources were in a better state her parents would find happiness. Through the years it seemed whenever her parents wanted something from her, they treated her kindly. However, most of the time they were thoughtless and mean spirited.

As an adult, Connie realized she could not relieve a person from their unhappy condition. Or give her sense of wonder to anyone; she can only share herself. For her own sake, she will have to break the chain of bondage—her conditioning. She should not allow others—even intimate relatives—to strip her spiritual backbone.

Example 2: Karma, Payback

Jill shared confidential information about a co-worker with her friend at work. To her surprise, her friend told their manager. Subsequently, Jill was fired. Before this incident, Jill accidentally saw the same manager in a sensual embrace with his secretary—he is married. Jill believes the manager was waiting for an excuse to fire her. Now she wants to call his wife so he too will feel the same pain he has inflicted on her.

By sharing confidential information, Jill made a huge error. Now she has to face the consequences of her actions. Getting back at someone will not undo what she has done. If anything, it will only close her heart and break her connection to move forward. Whatever the manager's karma is—it belongs to him.

REINCARNATION, MY TWIN BROTHER'S MESSAGE

On a bright sunny day, I walked past three empty fields. I thought of my twin brother and how he loved the freedom of being outside whether he was on land or at sea. It had been a few weeks since his passing and I sensed he was trying to communicate with me. I felt sad. I missed him so much. I took a few deep breaths and replaced my sadness with his love. I looked at the fields. I felt he was everywhere—a part of everything. In that moment, it seemed as though he was walking beside me.

Instantly, I felt we were spiritually linked together. Our connection was definitely alive. I heard his gentle voice. He told me everything he had been part of—including me—and our relationship as I knew it was gone.

He mentioned I sensed him at these fields because they represented his freedom—his energy. Now our relationship is on many dimensional levels connecting us further than our physical life. And that place is powerful. It is the Godhead where all existence flows as one.

I asked him about reincarnation. "Is it true people are reborn, and then recognize each other in the next lifetime? Do we form negative relationships due to a weakness we experienced from a previous lifetime (karma)?"

He answered my question with a balanced tone of "Yes and No." He said," Once a person passes away he or she no longer exists as you know it. The life we live is our first and last. For instance, think of your spirit as motion—similar to the movement of the water in a stream. We cannot put our foot in the same water twice.

I commented, "But what about people mentioning they recognize a person from another lifetime. How they feel utterly comfortable with a certain someone."

Donald quickly intervened, "They feel comfortable because their spirit's energy recognizes how the other person connects with him or her. It is the same sensation when one gravitates toward a person's weakness.

One cannot make excuses for his or her actions in life. If so, it is an indication that something is misleading his or her heart. In the physical world, there is always something or someone to help individuals through difficult times just as there is always someone to bring individuals down.

Many people feel it is not fair to be born with a disability, impoverished, or have a dysfunctional family. They feel they should have the chance to experience wealth, be applauded for a talent, beauty, have a wonderful relationship, or loving family.

If one has an illness, one will have to take the correct steps to take care of the illness. If one has a dysfunctional family, one will have to make an adjustment to survive and make the best of the circumstance.

So many perceptions are relative and the trappings of the mundane world easily place us in the state of suffering.

One's life has nothing to do with privilege or anything else. Sentient beings are so into measurement—a Caste/Class system. I cannot accentuate this enough. Observe the diversity around you. Stop measuring yourself against another person or something else.

Experience all losses and lessons gained. Do not allow mental states to harden your heart—live life to the fullest. Notice the second chances staring you in the face. Stop wishing and hoping you will be vindicated in your next lifetime. All you have is today.

Hmm... Let me put it this way. Our spirit is molded into a container—one's body. The harmonic energy field surrounding the spirit (a part of the spirit—individuality) is endless and deep. It is larger and more dimensional than anything one could imagine. I am not even considering the vastness of the universal energy. To measure the spirit against the trapping of the physical world is impractical.

For instance, in the pragmatic world, we physically change as we grow older and our priorities also change. When one is nine years old, one views watching a particular movie as important. When one is thirty-five years old, one speculates about having a good retirement plan as important. When one is eighty, one considers having good health and the quality to life to be important. This is a sentient being reality but not one's whole reality.

Consider the daylilies in your back yard. Daylilies have a bulb—a seed which produces flowers each season. In the summer, those flowers blossom, wither, and die. The bulb and the flower is not the same as before—even though at first glance it may look the same. The flower lived its life. The next daylily has its own life and like the flower before it will be vulnerable to disease, bugs, and weather conditions. Who knows it may not survive.

Contemplate nature. Nature is a force that sustains the planet. It is natural, yet changes daily. It does not repeat itself. We are not any different than the flowers. Everything is a part of the consciousness that binds all things together."

I partially understood Don's explanation. I said, "In another word, I will not become Doris Ann Bridgehouse again? I will become part of the mix like everyone else—such as Einstein, Emerson, Gandhi, and even Hitler. That reminds me, what about the special people in the world; the people who are unique and help mankind?"

Donald pursued his point. "That is a great question,. Through one's choice, everyone has a chance to make the world a better place. It is not about charisma, appearance, education, how much money one has in the bank, or how easy or tough their life is. Opportunity or the lack of it has nothing to do with our connection to each other.

"Recognize your power. If you wish for more, make it so. Recognize spiritual individuality and graciously open your energy field. Recognize those who love you. Listen to another's heart. Find yourself. Find yourself in another person. If you cannot do this today, how will you do it later?"

I sighed trying to absorb it all. I stated, "To be honest, I am beginning to feel upside down. It seems so confusing."

I felt Donald move from our connection. His last words were potent.

"Live in the mystery. Believe whatever provides comfort. Discover your own path and fulfill your fondest dreams. Do not get caught in the web of dissolution for that path leads to nowhere. Also, whatever your religious conviction, (the same for those who do not have one) honor the people who have given you their love and allow their teachings to become an example for yourself."

PART IV

HARMONY

IN A MOMENT

Thirsty for the new
A moment honors the undiscovered
Shaping our hearts and widening our existence

Formless images stretch
The foundations of the already
Breaking forth
Sharply cutting
Cutting into one's fantasy
Destroying the road once traveled
Announcing all emptiness

Forsaking the past
Judgments lift
Fear loses its power

Behold the visions sleeping
Where the unexpected lie
Free our spirits to taste the golden moment
So we may embrace the image of reflection
And enjoy the insights hidden in this sacred space.

Chapter XVII

Past mistakes were lessons learned.
In the present moment, you have
already passed the test—no judgment.

Balance

In a natural state, balance does not have an extreme. There is a letting go while one makes a commitment to the middle. It is a manifestation without sides. When we are balanced, there are no empty, destructive or isolated sensations to experience.

Allowing our conditioning or ego to rule our lives makes balance impossible to achieve. The first step toward achieving balance is recognizing the messages you give to yourself. The second step toward balance is recognizing the messages you give to others.

Exercise:
Ask a person about his or her day—listen intently. Make a point to give someone a compliment. Show com-

passion. By practicing these simple exercises, you will feel balanced.

Maturity versus Immaturity

Maturity is when individuals take responsibility for their actions or their lack of action. Mature people understand that the decisions they make impact their lives. Immature individuals are peripheral and indifferent to their sense of focus. They are not aware that their actions predetermine their joy or suffering.

Example: Maturity

Kevin and Karen are newlyweds. Each of their in-laws feels jealous of their children's affections toward their extended family. Weekly, the two families wrestle for Kevin and Karen's undivided attention. The peak of their troubles became prominent during the holiday preparations. On their first holiday, each family expected the young couple to show their presents in their home, first. The squabbling and disharmony made visiting both families intolerable.

The young couple cannot allow themselves to be caught in the middle of someone else's conflict. It is the season for them to make a decision based on their comfort level. Otherwise, they will lose their sense of unity.

Criticism and Constructive Criticism

Criticism in itself is an expression of someone's opinion of how something should be. There are people who criticize because they live their life with assumptions. They believe their ideas are true and fault finding is justifiable. This type of critical superiority is self-applauding. Their heart disconnects from others—control is more important than bonding.

For example, I know a young couple who has been married ten years. They yell and put each other down, daily. The have callused their marriage and mentally and emotionally "check out." Oddly enough, they have no idea how detached they have become.

People have common ways they respond to criticism. The shutdown type will turn silent. He or she will do his or her own thing by charting a course through the home that will not intersect with anyone. The other partner may slam doors, lob countercharger, and close himself or herself off emotionally by bonding with the computer or television. Both attitudes show resentment.

Disarm and deflect defensiveness with honesty. Demand nothing. Accept the truth. Notice if your partner knows how much you are hurting. Question whether he or she cares enough to change the situation.

For the sake of connecting to others, do not allow the absence of understanding, inattention, and pride to cloud your perception—stay poised. Behaving negatively to damage another person has a recoiling effect. In reality, when someone is showing a critical manner toward others that person is revealing the scope of his or her insecurities.

Constructive criticism is also an opinion, although there is a gentle thought behind the criticizer's position. The criticizer's temperament shows impartiality. He or she explores a thought, but never reveals a condescending or condemning tone. No one is keeping score. When one shows a positive attitude toward another person, he or she reflects intimacy.

Example 1: Criticism, Biting Conversation

During an impromptu visit, my uncle visited his son and daughter-in-law. During the visit, his son and daughter-in-law spoke about his wife with severe criticism. As ill luck would have it, my uncle went home and repeated every word to his wife. Now my aunt does not want to go to any holiday gatherings—she feels perturbed and embarrassed.

I told my aunt some of her anger should be directed toward my uncle. He had no right to deliver such a painful message. Sometime during the visit someone became a motormouth and in the heat of the negative discussion others followed. I did not hear that my uncle tried to stop the biting conversation.

My aunt needs to take steps to correct the issue the best she can. I suggested they have a family conference at a restaurant—a neutral ground. Relay what she heard to clear the air. Ask for an apology and mention she does not want to talk about it again. Start anew. Maybe before the holiday season she could ask her son and his family to visit. It would break the ice and help everyone to move on.

Example 2: Criticism Versus Compliments

Kara's boyfriend criticizes her often. When she confronts him, he tells her she does not handle criticism well. He feels his perceptions are made from perfection. She needs to observe her boyfriend's attitude, question if his criticism out-weighs his compliments. Criticizing how one folds the clothes, packs the dishwater, vacuums, or cooks does not belong in a loving relationship.

The happiest couples lovingly and constructively criticize each other for their companion's best interest. For example, "Dear you are eating with your mouth open."

"Sweetheart, you are speaking too loud." Note the message is sent with much warmth and kindness. The other half of the couple does not feel he or she is being ridiculed.

Example 3: Criticism, Damaging Relationship

My girlfriend's daughter, Patsy, became romantically involved with a co-worker. However, he has been living with another woman for five years. Everyone in Patsy's family has tried to convince her to give up this man, but she insists he plans on leaving his other girlfriend someday.

Her mother does not understand her daughter's logic. She was raised with awareness that when you were with a person and you felt good about yourself—that was a good thing. But if you felt worse when you are not with that person it was a clear indicator something is wrong with the relationship. People get lonely and sometimes depressed. Mentally, Patsy seems like she is under a gray cloud that even makes a negative situation look terrific.

No one can talk anyone out of a sour decision. I told my friend to lovingly support her daughter and mention how she will be there for her. It is likely one day this self-absorbed man will move to another conquest. Hopefully, before that time she will have seen the light and grown out of this damaging relationship.

Exercise:

If you feel a strong need to give someone constructive criticism, dwell on the impact Take a deep breath. Hold your breath for a few seconds. Be aware and question yourself before you make a critical statement to anyone. For no matter how lightly you express yourself, there is a possibility an individual may not be filled with gratitude.

THE BRAIN AND INTELLIGENCE

The brain is an organ in our cranium composed of gray and white matter—connecting our central nervous system. It is the receptacle of our consciousness, thoughts, memories, and emotions. The brain is earth base. It is where we store knowledge in order to relate to the physical world. Intelligence does not come from the brain.

For instance, tapping into the connection—the central part of being what I call the universal flow is where intelligence lies. Many well known philosophers may call it something else—MIND. True intelligence is taking one's knowledge and mixing it with purpose and then sprinkling it with a meditative silence.

How does one renew his or her self to form a greater intelligence? Simplicity rules intelligence. Break old patterns. Understand yourself. Build new learned pathways and take a cognitive step out of your square box. Move toward an action that is mixed with compatibility and compassion. By perceiving the interconnectedness of the world, one automatically jump starts positive changes in his or her life—intelligence.

Questions:

Do you take your known facts mixed with reason and share that pertinent information in order to expand the world? Are you living life through your own one-sided conversation?

• Helping someone to take care of a problem is far more effective than going out of your way to "fix things."

Example: Finding the Path to True Intelligence

Barbara was poor as a child. Her family lived on a tight budget and her wardrobe consisted of a friend's older sister's clothing. She never said anything to anyone, but daily, she would seethe when she wore the hand-me-downs.

As an adult, she is a clothing shopaholic. Secretly, she still feels she does not belong, and the hunt for new clothes gives her (ego) a temporary lift. She has clothes in her closet she has never worn.

Through the years, Barbara has made a scar on her brain pathways that keep her in this blinding habit. In order for Barbara to change her path of destruction, she needs to look at her closet and set limits for herself. She could place her clothes on her bed and separate the clothes she loves and the clothes that are just okay—new or otherwise.

The clothes that are iffy must go back to the store or she could give them to her favorite charity. The clothes she decides to keep she could coordinate, reorganize, and appreciate. She could admire what she owns and give herself positive affirmations to reinforce her new outlook.

When she feels weak and she yearns to buy new clothes, she could mindfully occupy herself with a positive deed. Possibly, she could even finish a chore that she has been putting off. Breaking negative pathways takes practice. The upshot: she will renew her outlook on life.

CHAPTER XVIII

Think differently, and use kind words to express yourself.

LIFE'S WAKE-UP CALL

Have you ever noticed the impact of life's wake-up call—a powerful insight? This wake-up call immediately changes one's previous views. In a physical sense, the manifestation is similar to a Zen monk hitting a meditator with a stick when he or she begins to slouch.

For example, the wake-up call could be connected to a relationship perception, a shadow lifts, an unknown talent emerges, one has a religious experience, or anything that changes our habitualness.

Give yourself an empathic overview. Do not waste the impact of a wake-up call—often missed. Seize an unexpected moment through observance. Feel the shifting edges directing you toward a new thought pattern. Treasure and value the moment. Enjoy the unexplained. If you do not believe me, ask an elderly person if at one time he or she has overlooked an insight at a pivotal moment in order to nurse a fixed psychological idea.

Example: Wake-up Call

Scotty and Charlie met each other in elementary school and became fast friends. Through their youth they were inseparable. Scotty went to a local college. Charlie went to an Ivy League college from which his father had graduated. Even though they lived a few hundred miles apart, they kept in touch and visited each other often. As a matter of fact, Charlie introduced Ann Marie, Scotty's fiancée, to him in their junior year.

After the young men graduated from college, they started a business together. In seven years the business grew into a huge success. Suddenly, at a client's business meeting and with bravado in his voice, Charlie announced he was planning to resign and retire to Tahiti.

Scotty was stunned Charlie did not speak with him first. When the meeting was finished, he grabbed Charlie's arm and asked to borrow the client's conference room. While they walked toward conference room, Scotty racked his brain.

For the past few months Charlie had been acting erratic, peculiar, and evasive. He presumed he may have had a fight with Ann Marie or he was not feeling well. Scotty made several attempts to have a serious conversation with Charlie, but he nonchalantly brushed him aside.

There was something odd about Charlie. Something he could not put his finger on. Then he remembered about four years ago Charlie had the same persona when he had lost a great deal of money gambling.

In the conference room, Charlie's legs twitched and he avoided Scotty's eyes. While Scotty spoke, Charlie tapped his fingers on the table. Scotty mentioned he was going to pour himself a cup of coffee, he asked Charlie if he would like a cup.

As Scotty walked back with the coffee cups in hand, he caught a glimpse of Charlie. He saw him as another person. A person he did not know. Within that instant, a lightening bolt struck him. He knew without doubt Charlie was leaving for reasons that had nothing to do with retiring. Suddenly, he felt there could be a possibility that Charlie embezzled money from their company,

Scotty had a wake-up call. This intense moment changed his view of Charlie–a "what is" moment. Scotty is going to have a heart-to-heart conversation with Charlie. Under these new conditions, Scotty has changed his perception of their relationship.

DESTINY'S DELIVERANCE

Do you believe in destiny? Do you sense there are certain directions you must take throughout life and you will not be able to change that direction? Before we go any further, I would like define the word destiny; Destiny is the seemingly supernatural, inevitable, or necessary succession of events.

Destiny has nothing to do with choices. It is a compressed time bubble within our energy field—holding a component of surprise. We somehow tap into it and mold it as we live. Destiny is elusive and mystifying. It moves individuals into unplanned territory.

Before a destiny's deliverance, there is a lull—a melancholy feeling—that makes individual's feel blah. There is an uncertainty. One minute you are clear, and then within an instant, your mind is foggy. You may even become tearful without reason.

You feel discontent and disconnected. There is an eerie sense of not belonging—almost as if you were watching a movie of your life. You may not care about the events that normally affect you. This vague indecisive persona will likely befuddle your friends and relatives. They will not understand why you seem detached.

It will not be easy—in the state of confusion and indifference—to take advantage of this new energy source. Timing is important. Practice awareness and allow yourself to move forward. During this juncture, you will need plenty of rest. Maybe fast a little and make an effort to be in a quiet place. Sometimes, depending on one's habits, individuals may find themselves craving certain foods they usually did not care for.

When destiny's deliverance touches you, you will feel a surge of energy. It will happen suddenly without any warning. Destiny's deliverance is usually connected to a new idea or a surprise message. You could meet someone unlike anyone else you have known before, possibly observe a present relationship from another viewpoint or change an outlook at one hundred and eighty degrees.

Destiny transforms you into another person. You feel fresh and new—a rebirth. You may think of the old cliché, "If I knew then what I know now, my life would have been easier." Do not go there; never allow your ego to outshine this stirring event.

Take a moment, to look into the mirror. See yourself for the first time. Speak out loud, "I am thankful that my past experiences helped me build dimension to my life— now I can experience a whole new me.

You may wonder how a wake-up call and destiny's deliverance differ. A wake-up call is a powerful instant recognition about something that was necessary for you to understand. Destiny's deliverance can be an emotional or physical event that happens beyond what was initially visible. An intuitive individual may notice there is a lull in the air just before an out-of-the-ordinary situation occurs.

Example: Destiny's Deliverance

It took nine years for Shepard to finish his mystery novel. He self-published and knocked on doors to sell his book at local stores. Some local stores would not give him the time of day—he never begrudged those who did not, but honored those who took a chance on him.

In a matter of months, his goal took him out of state. Slowly and surely his book has infiltrated the market. But sometimes Shepard felt his time was wasted. It seemed that his effort was in vain. The few books he did sell did not justify the time he put into it. He knew there was nothing like this book anywhere and he wondered why it was taking so long for the book to catch on.

Then one day without warning someone he knew asked him to appear on a television show. Suddenly, he had a chance to tell the world why he wrote his book and how the contents of the book would touch others. He could not have planned this outcome. It just happened—destiny's deliverance.

HEALING

Healing does not mean a betrayal or a traumatic event will disappear from one's psyche or one's thoughts. There is no such thing as being miraculously cured. Healing means you have the energy to live again, to trust again, and to start from the beginning. In life, we build upon our train wrecks. We glue and patch ourselves the best we can, and then we move to a better place. A place where we love and show kindness to ourselves and others.

It will not be easy, but try not to give in to your misery. Ask your spirit how a situation can be tempered. Shake off negative energy by doing something positive (see Chapter XIX, "Meditation and Space").

HEALTH AND NATURE CONSCIOUSNESS

The natural order in the physical world is as simple as walking down a road and picking up a pebble. We must be conscious of our proper health and hygiene. The stronger our body feels the stronger our spirit can respond to life. Even if one has a health disability, honoring the body gives the spirit strength—perpetual connection. Make an effort to consume nutritional foods, vitamin supplements, and regularly exercise by walking, swimming, or working out at a gym.

Doctors guide us, but we are responsible to listen to our body's intricate necessities. As soon as we feel our health deteriorate, we must intervene and make sure that the health symptoms can be corrected through medicines or homeopathic therapies.

When we worry about our health we bring more worry to ourselves—ego-based. This is the time to flood the mind with positive health messages. Picture your body healthy and watch it heal. Recognize your body is you and any negative message is your ego trying to pamper itself.

Realize one's essence is as large as the ocean, as beautiful as the warm sun, and as mysterious as the shadows on the moon. It embodies every lifeform and inanimate object without any defined edges. We are like the reeds in the wind. The wind does not change the reeds. They bend from side to side forming a oneness with the winds' life force.

Bend with life's ambivalence. For we can no more move from the foundations of who we are than a plant can change its roots. We are on this earth and must function in connection to others as the earth functions with the elements of nature. Feel the power. Nothing is separate. We are not any more separate from the trees than the trees are from the earth or the earth from the universe—it all exists as one.

Experiment wearing one of nature's many colors. Observe the colors that give you a natural glow.

NATURE'S COLOR CODES

Gold	Brilliance	Seek Reality	Strong Willed
Silver	Romantic	Carefree	Observant
White	Time to Reflect	Truthful	Serenity
Red	Energy	Aggressive	Sensual
Orange	Material Oriented	Attentive	Curious
Yellow	Cheerful	Youthful	To Learn
Green	Health	Money	Busy
Blue	Spiritual	Longing	Aloft
Purple	Royalty	Grandiose	Acceptance
Brown	Earthy	Stubborn	Stability
Black	Leap of Faith	Concentration	Warrior
Charcoal	Artistic	Friendly	Clever
Gray	Simple	Sedate	Contemplative
Cream/Ivory	Alert	Talkative	Patience
Pink	Passionate	Free	Open to Suggestion
Peach	Mysterious	Good Memory	Spiritual
Garnet	Rooted	Deep Awareness	Expressive
Burgundy/Wine	Sharp Mind	Excellent Memory	Independent
Glitter/Metallic	Clarity	Multi Dimensional	Creative

Chapter XIX

Your bounties of greatness are forever expanding—enjoy.

Meditation and Space

Meditation definition: a devotional exercise leading to a contemplative reflection—a stillness, a silence. Think of a meditation of as a space devoid of energy. The space is neither dark nor light. And it does not have a beginning or an ending. The type of meditation you practice does not matter as much as taking a few minutes to quiet your mind. Meditation will help you to raise your sense of awareness—allowing you to notice another human being is not a threat to your ego.

The benefit of meditation helps our physical health as well as our mental health. Best of all it gives us a moment to stop and shut out obsessive worries. In this space, we find a positive link with ourselves. I cannot express the importance of allotting a slice of time to honor one's day. In reality, we practice meditation without thinking about it. Prayers and even menial tasks are forms of meditation, being aware of our existence, by listening, and by being cognitive of our actions one ultimately practices meditation.

The more you meditate the easier and smoother it will become. Do not place expectations on the results or put time limits on this exercise. Meditation is not about time or what you do as much as how you do it. For example, the days you feel you do not have enough time to formally meditate, step back and take a deep breath. Hold your breath until you fill your lungs with air. Release your breath through your mouth, slowly—feel your warm breath. Contemplate on the clouds, a tree, a flower, or anything that gives you a sense of peace. Appreciate each day with a gesture of thank you. Respect yourself as well as others. Smile! Smile! Smile! Relish someone helping you. And be open to new ideas. Always be mindful of how you are treating others and how others are treating you.

Below are some basic meditation techniques. They will take a little preparation, and if need be, you may modify them to your liking. For more meditation techniques, visit your local book store or library.

MEDITATION RITUALS

Meditation 1:

MEDITATION 101

Before you begin to meditate, you should feel slightly hungry, but not famished. Wear comfortable clothing. Walk around your house and look for a space that feels safe—relaxed. The room could be dark or well lit. Especially for first time meditators, turn off the telephone and music. The answering machine should be shut off as well.

After a few meditation sessions, you will find that noises and other distractions do not disrupt you. If you the nervous type, slowly drink some water before you begin. Recite an affirmation (one word) or a mantra until you feel comfortable.

The space you pick should be devoid of clutter. If you cannot get away from clutter, place a tablecloth or a piece of material over the area. Or position a chair away from the clutter—toward a corner. You could also look out a window. This is my rule. As you understand yourself better, do whatever works for you.

Sit in a comfortable position, either on the floor with a pillow under you or in a straight-back chair. If you are in a chair, plant your feet firmly on the floor. Stare at an icon until you feel relaxed. An icon could be anything from a candle flame, a picture of a loved one, a religious figure, a nature scene, or any object that gives you a sense of peace.

Concentrate on your breath. Inhale. Feel the air seep through your nostrils. Fill your diaphragm. Exhale through your mouth. Recognize your existence. Repeat as needed—at least twice. If you prefer, you may half close or close your eyes. When thoughts pop into your head, observe those thoughts. Watch them as if you were watching a movie. Do not make a shrine out of a situation. If necessary, recite a one word affirmation.

Focus on the space between your nose and your eyebrows—sometimes called the third eye. Some people may picture a light in this area—God's eye—where clear decisions lay. Inhale and hold your breath. As you are holding your breath, imagine you are writing the number 3 on a blackboard. You do not have to see it as much as believe it to be there. Release your breath through your mouth, slowly. Inhale again and hold your breath. Imagine writing the number 2, and then release your breath. Inhale again and hold your breath. Imagine writing the number 1. Release your breath.

The number 1 represents you. Picture the one glowing, growing taller, wider, and larger. You can make it as tall and as wide as you like. Listen to your heartbeat. Feel your limbs, stomach, and all parts of your body. Be aware of your senses. Stay in this state as long as you wish. If your mind wanders, look at the number one again—make it grow and glow with a brilliant light. End your meditation by inhaling, hold, exhale, and slowly count forward 1... 2... and 3.

Meditation 2:

GUIDED MEDITATION

Follow the meditation technique 1 by counting 3... 2... and 1—backward. Do not forget to inhale, hold and exhale slowly. Feel the life in your warm breath. Listen to your heartbeat. In your mind, you can be anywhere you would like to be. Picture yourself in a scene where you feel safe and free from bondage. Think of the sun shining. Think of snow falling. Think of sitting in front of a fire. Picture the waves in the ocean, follow the ripples in a country stream, the beauty of a dense forest, or any place that gives you joy.

Free yourself. Walk into the warm cloud of the unknown. This newfound balance will give you an intelligence that is bound to dissipate your illusions and—in turn—give you clarity. End your meditation by inhaling, hold, exhale, and slowly count forward 1... 2... and 3.

Meditation 3:

ADDICTION MEDITATION

I like this meditation technique. I find it helpful with addictions. Take a deep breath feel the air seep through your nostrils. Exhale through your mouth. Do this three times or until you feel relaxed.

Picture your addiction in your third eye (see meditation 1 for explanation). Embrace it with all your being. Name one reason why your addiction means everything to you. Think of the addiction as a loved one. Someone you cannot live without. Place the addiction in a sail boat and watch it sail toward the open sea.

Take a deep breath and inhale and exhale. Do not rush this process—sincerity matters. Now name four reasons why you no longer crave your addiction. While you are naming the reasons, feel the power. After you feel clear, imagine soft foamy waves slowly pushing the sailboat out to sea further.

When the sailboat is in the middle of the immense ocean, suddenly, a beautiful and powerful tsunami drives the sail boat to the bottom of the ocean's floor. Watch the sail boat become filled with sand until it is entirely buried. Feel how your addiction will lay at the bottom of the ocean forever. You are free from your wrenching habit. If need be, repeat this meditation technique. Under most circumstances, your spirit has the power to eradicate your problem.

Meditation 4:

CLEANSING MEDITATION

Attempt to take a new approach and outlook on life. If possible spend a day at home alone, without any distraction. Shut off the telephone, television, radio, and computer. Live in complete silence for one hour. If you cannot manage one hour without some type of noise, try a half hour or less. This practice will help you recognize how the ego keeps your monkey mind occupied.

The longer you experience silence, the better. Watch your ego how it tries to fill itself with thoughts and memories. Pay close attention to your belief patterns. How do your beliefs make you feel? Question the absurdity of your illusions.

Meditation 5:

ACTION MEDITATION

Take a pen and a pad with you and find a relaxed space either inside or outside that speaks to you. Inhale and exhale with two deep breathes. Express how you feel about yourself. Be brutally honest and do not rush this process. Write in lower case letters the person you think you are. Then write in upper case letters the person you want to become. It is imperative you feel peaceful and comfortable with your new self.

Place the pad or paper near a favorite chair, bathroom mirror, the refrigerator, or a cabinet door that you open often. Keep the writings in sight for a few weeks or months. You determine the time limit.

This meditation technique will give you a greater awareness of self. And it is imperative you make sure your daily projections match your actions. Think about it. If it took you years to be the person you are now, what difference will it make to take weeks or months or years to be in a better place?

Do not place a chronological time limit on feeling better about yourself. Enjoy the fact that each conscious moment releases you from the past and helps you focus on the present. Do not allow pessimism and negative thoughts to hinder your process.

Meditation 6:

FREEING MEDITATION

Investigate why you are driven to hold onto psychological pain (see Chapter XII, "Psychological Moment"). Before you meditate, place a treasured keepsake in your lap—a crystal, stone, or anything that is small and holds a positive meaning for you.

Sit in a room alone—preferably dark. Take two deep breathes, hold your breath for a moment, and exhale through your mouth. Feel the breath's warmth. Become part of your breath. Feel yourself slip into a silent place.

Now write on a piece of paper how a particular sticking-point muddles your life. A short sentence will do. Feel the scars connected to your pain. Do not point your finger or blame anyone. Search within. Observe your thoughts. Anytime you feel irritated concentrate on the object you are holding in your lap until you feel safe. If need be, inhale and exhale three deep breaths.

After you feel relaxed, slowly crumple the paper. As you crumple the paper say to yourself, "I release myself from (fill in the blank)." Tear the paper in small pieces, place them in your hand, and separately throw each piece of the paper in the garbage—feel the release.

Ask the power of your insights to take you to a better place. Before you know it, you will be receiving a new strength. Some sort of message will reveal something to you. If you cannot comprehend the knowledge you received, wait... you will know what you must know at the right moment.

Try this exercise daily for one week. You will feel stronger and your conflict will become weaker. Slowly, the darkness of control and conflict will not have the same hold on you. Know your psychological pain will eventually dissipate as you open yourself to a new way of thinking. Sometimes the pains from the past are removed immediately—as a long shot, give yourself a month.

During a healing process resist putting your life on hold—have fun and keep active. Even though you may have a heavy burden or responsibility that does not mean it is time to stop living. Change your attitude. Take yourself out on a date and do something you have never experienced.

Attend a book signing. Look in the newspaper. There are many events going on. Join a church function. It does not even have to be your denomination. Many churches have interesting programs. Meet people. Visit an obscure park. Visit a meditation group or try a new meditation technique. Exercise, walk to a new place, study new subjects, travel, or join a club. Ideas are life's playground—enjoy.

For those who are shut in, open your mind. Use your imagination. There are endless ideas in the world waiting for your discovery—the Internet helps. Love your life and be comfortable with the person who looks at you in the mirror. Believe me. Your spirit will show you how to go for it.

Meditation 7:

NATURE MEDITATION

This is a nature meditation technique. In your backyard, a park or anywhere there are open spaces, find a rock, tree or space that gives you solace. Sit and practice the 3... 2... and 1 meditation exercise. Exhale and inhale at least twice—slowly. Allow your breath to flow through your mouth. As you are doing this, feel the earth, the air, the breeze and enjoy the sounds around you. Become one with these things.

Repeat out loud slowly, "I am in a better place and I love the space I am in. I am no longer making (name a situation) an important part of my life. I am moving on." Do not waste time on rehashing why and what for. Fly like a bird and explore the world. Feel the universal energy flow through all things. End the meditation by inhaling, hold, exhale, and slowly count backwards 1... 2... and 3.

Meditation 8:

FORGIVENESS MEDITATION:

As I mention in Chapter XI, forgiveness is an action. It is not an exercise to "jolly" reality out of the moment. If you are seeking forgiveness, write a letter or make a telephone call and express your apology. Do not worry about losing your dignity and self-respect. Free yourself.

If a person has passed away, write a letter expressing how you feel. Make a funeral ritual by putting the letter in a bucket. Burn the letter. As you burn the letter, place your hands together (in a prayer fashion). Ask for forgiveness. Speak out loud. "I forgive myself and I would like (name individual) to forgive me."

Unclasp your hands and shake them with your palms facing away from you. Take a deep breath. Forgive yourself. Douse the ashes with water. Empty the contents on the ground and cover it will a layer of dirt. Leave the scene without looking back.

If you do not live in an area where you can burn a piece of paper, place a slip of paper in a dish and tear it up in tiny pieces. Note it is better to tear it than cut it with scissors. After you feel comfortable, place the message into a bag, seal it tight, and throw it away. Do not bring the message back into your home. If you feel inclined, ask a trusted friend to join you in the forgiveness ritual.

Meditation 9:

CLARITY MEDITATION AND OTHER PRACTICES

Similar to the above meditation count slowly backward 3... 2... and 1, and then meditate on a particular subject. It could be anything. Maybe you need clarity about a dysfunctional relationship, insecurity, finances, the feeling you never have enough, your career, or to expunge something that is holding you back from living a peaceful life.

Through meditation, you can reflect on those matters or just stop for a moment to quiet your mind. End your meditation by inhaling, hold, exhale, and feel the warmth of your breath as you slowly count 1... 2... and 3.

If you cannot find the time to clear your mind of a certain neurosis, take a moment to inhale and exhale. Stare in the mirror at the center of your eyes. Feel your warm breath flow through your mouth. Stay in this position until you feel comfortable.

Ask yourself what makes you feel divided or insecure with others. Say your thoughts out loud repeating them several times. Search within. Allow your spirit to look back at you. Recognize that the person looking back at you is a whole person. At this point, your ego will be at its weakest.

Bless your awareness, and do not worry about being everything to everybody. You are your own guide. Note someone else's baggage cannot take anything away from you. For individuals who need to release themselves from something, practice the above meditation exercise.

ANOTHER MEDITATION PRACTICE

Write a few sentences or paragraphs to express a doubt, a fear, a current block, insecurity, anything about a belief, or relationship that holds you back. Do not read what you wrote; wait a week or more. Waiting will give you an objective viewpoint. Later make the changes in your life that have been challenged by your own words.

VISION BOARD

Take a blank piece of paper (the size does not matter) and place cut-out pictures with an inscription underneath. Each picture should reflect where you want to be. Make it upbeat and fun. For example, you could find a picture that resembles the new you, a destination for a trip, a promising goal, or any spiritual fulfillment that gives you joy. Place the vision board on your refrigerator or anywhere that you will see it often. As positive changes take place, revise the vision board.

LAWS OF FREEDOM

We travel through life searching fearlessly trying to discover our true-self. The energy flow connected to our spirit already instinctively knows how to walk on life's treasured path. Allow your spirit to move freely. The snippets below show an overview of how to love yourself and others and live a peaceful life. Do not worry if you trip up once in a while. You can only do your best.

Keeping The Connection Open

1. Live in the present moment.
2. Love yourself.
3. Feel how love surrounds you.
4. Learn to express yourself, often.
5. Tell someone you love him or her.
6. Provide an emotional cushion for the people around you.
7. Give someone your undivided attention.
8. Help a stranger.
9. Practice nonjudgment.
10. Admit regrets, and say you are sorry.
11. Become aware of the give-and-take in all relationships. Remember that compromise is a good thing.
12. Do not allow stressful moments to drag you down.
13. Do your best—the people who love you will understand.
14. Never lose oneself in another person.
15. Spiritual fulfillments are infinite—they activate themselves throughout life.

Giving And Receiving

1. Give compliments and receive compliments gracefully.
2. Spontaneously, give someone a gift.
3. Join others to celebrate their joy and happiness.
4. Perform unexpected favors.

Perfection

1. One's space belongs to oneself.
2. One's action validates the moment.
3. If you are doing something because you feel you have to, you are wasting your energy.
4. Do not allow your ego to control you. This happens as soon as you need approval or think you are grander and greater than anyone else.
5. One cannot be nagged into awareness.
6. When issues rise, see them from a new prospective and openly discuss all possibilities.
7. Your chances at perfection will never be as you have envisioned, but doing something to the best of your ability is a form of perfection.

Common Sense

1. If something you know is inappropriate, demonstrate through words and actions how a person should be treated. Absolutely no one deserves to be abused or neglected.
2. When there is a tragedy or someone passes away, try not to become paralyzed with inaction. Put yourself out there—even if you would rather take an easier route.
3. Never assume anything.
4. Take risks—ask questions. Try something new. Do not worry about looking stupid. No one on this earth knows everything.

5. Compassionately take care of your relationships. That is all one can do.
6. Detach yourself from someone else's learned concept of what should or should not be.
7. Do not allow the ego to support its importance.

Misery And Criticism—No Judgment

1. A person in pain seeks support but sometimes his or her life's trajectory may be influenced by depression. Moderately lend a listening ear. Realize no one can put a bandage on someone else's problems. When you provide someone with a solution and the individual refuses to pay attention, he or she will assume it is your job to fix the problem again.
2. Continual complaints about anything will not bring anyone to a better place.
3. How does one break the habit of listening to a person's complaints—I am not rich/smart/good/looking enough and I do not have a nice house/car/job? Ask what he or she is going to do about it.
4. When you find yourself thinking only if... my partner was a certain way I would be happier, you are essentially thinking your partner has failed you. No one can live up to someone else's ideals.
5. Eliminate pettiness.
6. Relate to people whose persona you admire.

Family Squabbles

1. Always try to approach a difficulty with helpful open arms.
2. Parents should be on the same page with their children's disciplinary actions.
3. Never argue in front of children.
4. Parents should never badmouth or volunteer disturbing details about each other to their children.

Emotional Withdrawal

1. Good friends would not complain about you to mutual friends or judge you for living the way that is comfortable for you.
2. Sometimes relationships may lose their intimacy such as when a lover may look elsewhere to fulfill his or her fantasies instead of searching within to deepen his or her present commitment.
3. One may be attracted to chaos or drawn to people who are unpredictable to feel alive.
4. Explore your environment and note how those traits enhance and connect with the quality of your character.
5. Look at all situations with openness.
6. When a friendship ends, one person is usually heartbroken. Below are some of the warning signs that a relationship may be ending.
a. One person acts erratic and dissatisfied with the status quo.
b. One person is preoccupied and/or short-tempered.
c. One person seems withdrawn or easily flustered.
d. One person is dismissive about his or her loved one's feelings, yet protective of their own.
e. One person has a mindset of thinking the situation is black and white while most situations are gray.

Desire And Detachment

1. Desire usually has a short fuse—wait out a "feeling." Detach yourself from the desire by questioning yourself: Will your desire bring you to a creative place? Will the desire put you at mental, financial, or physical risk? Are you harming another person by fulfilling a desire?
2. Having a partner does not mean you are joined at the hip.

3. Recognize your attachments whether it is to a person, idea, or thing.
4. Perceive the reality of "what is."

Focus On What Truly Matters

Feel safe in your own space before you commit fully to anyone or anything; otherwise you will feel dissatisfied.
1. Try not to revisit a complication. Sometimes it is best to wait and allow the dust to settle before one expands to another venue.
2. Be adaptable.
3. Share your improvements and setbacks with others.
4. Watch how you are living your life versus how you envision you are living your life.
5. Do not second-guess why family and friends do what they do. If in doubt, ask questions, then listen.
6. Do you live life through expectations?
7. Is there a give and take in your relationships?
8. Do you need a counselor? Counselors give people a chance to explore their motivations and behavior. They will not persuade a person to change a position; they know how to ask the right question to help a client figure out why he or she makes detrimental choices. Therapy is not easy. It is hard work and it takes courage to unwrap one's emotions and motivations when they seem to be encased in concrete.

Least Effort

1. Accept yourself and do not take someone else's opinion personally.
2. Take on a responsibility.
3. Defending a point of view is a waste of energy.
4. Fill your thoughts with positive affirmations.
5. Do not allow your ego to lead you.

6. Stop thinking about the past or projecting your thoughts toward the future. I always liked this quote by athletic coach and motivational speaker Allan Johnson: "The past is history. The future is a mystery. This moment is a gift. That is why this moment is called the present. Enjoy it."

7. When your actions and responsibilities reflect love, you experience the law of least effort.

8. If you chase an illusion or begrudge your responsibilities, you become a hungry ghost.

9. If someone is mistreating you, do not make room for negotiation.

Observe Life By Resetting Your Attitude

1. If you hate someone for a particular reason, realize it is the same thing in you that you hate.

2. If you blame someone for something, recognize you are blaming yourself also.

3. If you laugh at someone's belief, you are unsettled with your own belief.

4. If you find fault with the way a person wears their clothes or chooses to live their life, you are not settled with their own appearance or life.

5. If you feel you are right and the other person is wrong, you are close-minded. Every idea meets from a new point of view. One does not have to change as much as recognize everyone is different. And that is okay.

6. Each time life throws you something unexpected and you feel isolated reset your attitude button—enjoy.

Law Of Karma

1. Everyone lives his or her life by choice and every choice transforms an action into another choice—welcome to our polarized world.

2. When you make a decision that works to your advantage, you will feel a comfortable sensation throughout your mind and body—life's energy flows through you. If you make a decision that you know is wrong for you, you will feel uncomfortable.

3. Do not sleepwalk through life.

4. If in doubt about anything, wait until you are clear.

5. Love does not make a tangled web. If individuals are rebelling around you, smile and send love to their spirit—the connection within—and move forward. By knowing yourself, you can leave the maddening paradox of cause and effect behind you.

Purpose

Find your purpose in life. Relate to others with an open dialogue and listen with your heart.

1. Discover your true self, uniqueness, and talents.

   a. Write on a piece of paper your unique talent. If you do not think you have a talent, ask someone close to you to describe your talent. Above all, do not deny you have a talent—take an individual's word for it. Later, contemplate on those talents. See yourself as you have never seen yourself before.

   b. Volunteer your services to express your particular talent. This will promote self-satisfaction, give you security and help your talent to expand.

2. Selflessly, ask how to serve others.

Hypothesis

When we are not intelligently conscious, we place ourselves in a psychological stupor. Then we intentionally manifest levels of chaos with dramatic events to shock ourselves out of our sleepwalking existence. Hence when we open ourselves to love and to be loved we experience a flow—a bliss-fulness.

CONCLUSION – A LEGACY

In humanity's current state, some people believe their wealth and power gives them the influence to control the population with their viewpoints. Unfortunately, the gratification of a few can entice generations into believing they will receive the same privileges when they follow the master's example.

The days of recognition through one's material status is slowly changing. The public and the media require proven facts. Gone are the days where those who have written the laws do not have to follow the rules.

The millennium clears the worn-out ideas. The time has come to stop being slaves to the past. Let our legacy be measured by our respectfulness to ourselves, others, and the earth. It is here we feel the everlasting connection to the physical and spiritual worlds.

INDIVIDUALITY

Ask your spirit...
How to breathe in the fullness of the day
How to have the courage
To belong to yourself
How to break from the foolish
How to find equanimity
Do not think this is idealistic
Or a hopeless quest
Beneath life's changes
See the passing flux
With a determination and mindful eye
For it is through one's vision,
The wise becomes separate
Yet bonds with the group
It is then the spirit connects
Itself to joy and offers
An infinite energy
Where humanity's blessings live.